# SIMPLIFYING
## THE RAPTURE

# *SIMPLIFYING* THE RAPTURE

3 SCRIPTURAL TRUTHS THAT

SOLVE THE PUZZLE

by

Nelson Walters

***Ready For Jesus Publications*** (Wilmington, NC, 2018)
**ISBN-13: 978-0692055885**
**ISBN-10: 0692055886**

# CONTENTS

# CONTACT

The Gospel in the End Times Ministries

www.TheGospelInTheEndTimes.com

nelson@thegospelintheendtimes.com

# PART ONE:

## SIMPLIFICATION

# Chapter One

# WHY SIMPLICITY?

*"The unfolding of Your words gives light; It gives understanding
to the simple." (Psalm 119:130 NASB)*

The return of Jesus is one of the most universally anticipated and agreed upon events in all of Christendom. One day, Jesus will return from heaven to resurrect the dead in Christ, reward the righteous, punish the wicked, and rule the earth as its King. It is "The Day" all Christians look forward to.

And yet, the timing of when those glorious events will take place within the chronology of the "end times" is also the most *controversial* issue still facing the church. This difference of opinions has turned downright nasty at times, and the internet has exacerbated the viciousness of the disagreement. Name-calling and insults are commonplace. How can the event the Apostle Paul termed our "blessed hope" be the source of such unbrotherly behavior? The reasons are both emotional and financial. We will discuss why these factors are driving this Christian cultural debate in the next chapter.

However, these factors are only driving the *fervor* of the debate. The debate itself exists because the puzzle of Rapture timing hasn't been solved to everyone's satisfaction. No matter how Christians have tried to put the Scriptural pieces together, they haven't seemed to fit into one coherent picture. The Rapture dilemma is the equivalent of a 1000-piece, all-white puzzle. Imagine trying to put that together without a picture or colors to guide you! And the complexity of the dilemma has led to several, seemingly equally-valid positions being proposed; all of which claim to be the one true, biblical-based theory.

Oh, if we could only simplify the Rapture puzzle! If you are anything like me, you desire simplicity. "Just the facts, sir." "Let's cut to the chase and get to what is important." The reason I like simplicity is I'm simple! Maybe you are as well. And I want things *made* simple for me.

So why hasn't the Rapture puzzle been solved with simplicity? Why does it seem so complex?

"Simplicity does not precede complexity, but follows it."
—Alan Perlis

Alan Perlis, a scientist whose thought processes are much more complex than mine, nails it. We cannot have simplicity unless we first understand all the complexity of the issue. Only then can we break the issue down to its simplest components. $E=mc^2$ abridges the relationship between energy and matter in such a simple way that it only requires five characters to express it. In our "Twitter-centric, 142-character" world, we would still have 137 characters left to articulate the rest of our thought! And that is exactly what we desire for someone to do for us regarding the issue of the Rapture of the Church. Give us the $E=mc^2$ formula for the timing of the Rapture.

## LASER FOCUS

That desire for simplicity fuels the most common question I'm asked in radio interviews, "What is the *one* verse that proves Rapture timing?" Many have tried to answer it saying, "We don't know the day or hour, so the Rapture is pretribulational" or "Jesus returns after the tribulation of those days, so the

2

Rapture is post-tribulational." We desire simplicity, but unfortunately Scripture isn't quite *that* simple.

I'm not an Einstein or an Alan Perlis, nor am I able to reduce the Rapture Puzzle into five characters or a single verse, but this book does condense it into **three defining questions**. The Scriptural answers to these three questions will provide us with the simplicity we desire.

The reason this book is able to simplify the Rapture Puzzle is that complexity preceded it; just as Alan Perlis suggested. My previous book, ***Rapture: Case Closed?*** (Ready for Jesus Ministries, Wilmington, 2017), examined 147 separate Scriptural proofs of Rapture timing — nearly every proof used by proponents of every theory! It has been described as an "encyclopedia of Rapture proofs" by more than one expert in eschatology.

However, that book did not solve the Rapture puzzle for all of Christian culture, not because it was inaccurate, but partially because it was complex. *This* book takes the exact opposite approach. Rather than broadly looking at all the proofs of every theory, it focuses like a laser on the three primary evidences of Rapture timing: the three defining questions.

You have likely chosen to read this book because, like me, you desire simplicity . . . and truth. Hopefully you will find both.

## Why Simplicity "Works"

You may have looked ahead and read the three defining questions in "Section Two: Three Defining Questions" and been disappointed that your "favorite" Rapture proof was not included. You might be asking, "There are hundreds of questions about the Rapture, why did you choose these three?"

Let me answer your question by returning to our image of a 1000-piece, all-white jigsaw puzzle. What if the white pieces were each stamped with a number from 1 to 1000. And what if "piece one" attached to "piece two," etc., throughout the entire puzzle? How easy would assembling the puzzle be then? It would be much, much easier!

These three defining questions are the key to the entire Rapture puzzle. They are like numbering the pieces of an all-white jigsaw puzzle. They were chosen specifically because the answer to each one individually **proves** Rapture timing with biblical certainty, simplicity and without contradiction. In combination, there can really be no doubt about the puzzle's solution.

There is only one true Rapture answer. So if we prove that timing with 100% certainty from these proofs, the rest of the puzzle is much easier. You can then look at your favorite Rapture proof through the lens of already knowing what the correct answer is.

### "RABBIT HOLES"

But this is a very hard concept to accept, and frankly is the exact opposite approach to the one that Christians have taken in the Rapture discussion in our culture. If a person is presented with a truth that is "uncomfortable" to their preferred position, it is human nature to go down a "rabbit hole," a path that diverts attention away from the truth just presented. They say, "Yes, but what about this other proof . . .?" They try to distract the discussion away from the uncomfortable truth.

And that is why we haven't solved the Rapture timing debate to everyone's satisfaction up to this point. There are literally hundreds of verses that mention Jesus's return, and nearly every one of them has been used as a timing proof by proponents of the various theories. But frankly, I don't believe most verses that discuss the return of Jesus were ever intended to be used as evidence of Rapture *timing*.

As I stated earlier, my previous book looks at practically every proof of every theory. What I learned from that experience is that most verses about

4

Jesus's return are about something other than timing. Most are intended to teach *other* theological truths and mention Jesus's return primarily because it is what we should always be looking forward to and living for. So most verses about Jesus's return are a distraction to the Rapture timing debate.

That is why this book concentrates on only those passages that were *intended* to help us understand that timing. The Holy Spirit inspired these few biblical truths to give us that information, and that is where we need to concentrate our study.

Now that doesn't mean that all Bible verses that mention the return of Jesus don't have to be consistent with proper Rapture timing. They do. All of Scripture is consistent with itself and, when correctly understood, is without contradiction. But, those few scriptures that explicitly provide evidence of the timing should be our focus. And if we concentrate on *those* passages, we greatly simplify our search for truth.

As an example, let's say I wrote to you and told you I was coming to your house on Tuesday. If you and your friends got together and began to debate *why* I was coming and why that made it more likely for me to come on Wednesday, that would detract us from the truth that I was coming on Tuesday. Or if you and your friends debated the highway I was most likely to take and calculated the miles and the hours it would take me to travel it, that would also detract from the truth of *when* I was coming.

No, simplicity is the best approach. If I said, "Tuesday," I meant Tuesday. And the reason why I'm coming and the miles I must travel should harmonize with my clear and unambiguous statement, but they shouldn't be the focus. These other factors are "rabbit holes," not proofs.

So that is the approach this book takes. It concentrates on what is clear and biblically certain, and removes all the clutter of a hundred "rabbit holes"

5

that lead nowhere. If you're anything like me, you'll enjoy the clarity and convergence this methodology provides.

Each of the three defining questions have been chosen because when we answer them with Scripture, they clearly and simply define the timing of the Rapture. It's actually a much simpler puzzle than you have thought. So please, as you work through this book, do not be distracted by one or more of the hundreds of extraneous "rabbit hole proofs" you are already aware of. I realize it is human nature to do so, but resist the temptation. If you desire to learn more about your "favorite" proof, the aforementioned *Rapture: Case Closed?* contains thorough explanations of nearly all Rapture proofs.

### WHAT IF YOU'VE BEEN WRONG?

The discussion in the previous section brings up the painful possibility that you, the reader, may be mistaken about your current thinking on the Rapture. In chapter two, we will learn that, *by definition*, the majority of Protestant pastors are mistaken about the timing of the Rapture — regardless of what that timing turns out to be. Doesn't it stand to reason that the majority of our readers are mistaken as well? So I am asking a very difficult thing:

## Assume that you are WRONG about Rapture timing.

We are all mistaken about many things when we come to faith in Christ. But, as we explore the Word of God, we are to bring our thought processes into accord with that Word.

> Do not be conformed to this world, but be *transformed by the renewing of your mind*, so that you may prove what the will of God is. (Rom. 12:2 NASB, emphasis mine)

6

This is my "life verse," and it may be the life verse of many of you as well. But it is very challenging. The "renewing" of your mind is the *changing* of **your mind**. God expects us to change our viewpoints to come into agreement with his Word. If you are reading this book without a willingness, no, even an *expectation* that you may change your viewpoint on the Rapture, you are not truly seeking the truth.

I'm going to ask you another very, very difficult thing. Maybe one of the most challenging things you've done in your life. I'm going to ask you to pray to the Father to show you the truth about Rapture timing; not my truth or your truth, but HIS truth.

> Father in Heaven. Give us the wisdom through your Holy
> Spirit to see the truth in your Word. Then give us the strength
> to receive that Word and have it **change** our minds. Amen.

Prayer is the most powerful weapon in the world. If you just prayed that simple two sentence prayer, hang onto your hat, because the wind of God's Spirit is about to blow in your life and nothing may ever be the same again.

But, before we begin to examine the three defining questions in Section Two, in the next chapter, we'll define the terms we will use throughout the book and the main rapture theories at the heart of the controversy. Then after presenting them, we'll simplify them as well! Simplicity is understanding.

# Chapter Two

# Defining the Rapture

*"They will cry to the Lord because of oppressors, and he will*
*send them a Savior and a Champion, and he will deliver them."*
*(Isa. 19:20)*

A s we stated in the previous chapter, the return of Jesus is one of the most universally anticipated and agreed upon events in all of Christendom. Before we digress into the areas that the church disagrees about, let's define and delineate other areas of agreement, because there are many of them.

Most Christians are in agreement that man's rule over the earth will be brought to its conclusion at the end of a 7-year period Scripture refers to as the 70th Week of Daniel. But, our culture refers to that time as "**the Tribulation**." So for the sake of simplicity, we'll utilize the term our culture prefers even though it isn't found in Scripture.

Most Christians are also in concurrence that a **Great Tribulation** will occur in the latter part of that time period. Jesus said, "For then there will be a great tribulation, such as has not occurred since the beginning of the world until now, nor ever will" (Matt. 24:21 NASB). Tribulation (*thlipsis* in the Greek) means persecution or distress. Consequently, Jesus has informed us that a time of unparalleled distress and persecution is about to come upon the world prior to his return.

A majority of Christians also believe in an event called "**the Rapture**."

9

For the Lord Himself will descend from heaven with a shout, with the voice of the archangel and with the trumpet of God, and the dead in Christ will rise first. Then we who are alive and remain will be *caught up together* with them in the clouds to meet the Lord in the air, and so we shall always be with the Lord. (1 Thess. 4:16-17 NASB emphasis mine)

Most Christians expect Jesus to rescue his church in this way, by descending from heaven and then "catching up" or rapturing believers to meet him in the air. The Greek word translated "catching up" is *harpazo*. The Latin translation of this word, *rapio*, is the source of our English word "Rapture."

Finally, most Christians are also in agreement that after God rescues those who have had faith in Jesus, he will pour out his punishment on the unbelieving world. This punishment is known as **the Wrath of God**.

These four terms: **"the Tribulation," "the Great Tribulation," "the Rapture,"** and **"the Wrath of God"** are all you need to understand in order to make sense out of this book. If you have been intimidated by the complexity of the Rapture discussion, don't be. It can be made simpler than you think.

But as we also mentioned in the previous chapter, despite these areas of general agreement, the timing of the Rapture is one of the most hotly disputed issues by Christians. Specifically, this disagreement centers on whether the church will be safely rescued *prior* to the Tribulation or whether it will endure this challenging time. Obviously, this is of critical importance to every living Christian. Jesus gave a series of very detailed instructions for those that will enter that time. If current churchgoers endure that period, they will need to be prepared in order to obey Jesus's commands and overcome it.

Conversely, if churchgoers are going to be rescued first, the church needs to be aware of that as well. In that case, there will be no need for preparation, and efforts and resources should be applied elsewhere.

> **The entire strategy of our churches hinges on this single, crucial piece of information.**

And yet because of a lack of simplicity, every church and every Christian plan for the return of Jesus based on what they *think* is going to happen. But this is incredibly dangerous. The most important prophetic understanding in all of Christian history isn't something we should guess about. We need to know the answer with biblical certainty.

There was never a greater need for clarity and plainness in the last thousand years of church history. And that is the purpose of this book.

## WHY THE FERVOR?

In the previous chapter, we alluded to the fervor and down-right nastiness of the debate over this subject. Now that the central issue has been defined, the reasons for that fervor become plain.

The first reason is *emotional*. If the church truly faces the Tribulation period, believers will be subjected to starvation, persecution, and martyrdom at a rate never seen before in the history of the church. The death and torture of hundreds of millions of believers and their families is an emotional issue to say the least.

On the one side of this emotional debate are those who believe that even suggesting that Christians will enter the Tribulation will scare those within our pews unnecessarily. Potentially, it may literally scare churchgoers *out* of our pews. On the other side are those who are frightened that by ignoring Jesus's commands for that specific time period, leaders are leaving our churches totally unprepared for the greatest challenge in history. Fear is driving the emotions on both sides of the debate.

In addition to the emotional factor, *economics* plays a role in the Rapture debate. Many church and denominational leaders have spent their entire careers espousing one and only one view of the Rapture. If that view is proven wrong, ministries or even entire denominations may falter and fail. To say that multiple billions of dollars are at stake in the Rapture debate is *not* an understatement.

My previous book, ***Rapture: Case Closed?*** was sent to the 1000 most influential leaders of the American Church with the suggestion that a national academic forum be established to come to consensus on this issue. Despite hundreds of thank-you notes, calls, and comments, when it came to the issue of a national academic forum to actually resolve the issue, I heard . . . crickets.

The impact of these two factors, emotions and economics, means that realistically the church will never "solve" the Rapture puzzle because there are vested interests that **don't want the puzzle solved**. However, I trust that you are seeking truth, and in that spirit, we will continue to press on to simplify our understanding of the Rapture.

## RAPTURE TIMING THEORIES

There are five primary theories about *when* Jesus will return. And according to a recent Lifeway Research survey[1] of Protestant pastors, none of the five theories make up a majority of thought. If we turn this statistic around, it becomes apparent that a majority of Protestant pastors are currently ***incorrect***

---

[1] "Pastor Views on the End Times," Lifeway Research, last modified 2016, accessed Dec. 24, 2017, http://lifewayresearch.com/wp-content/uploads/2016/04/Pastor-Views-on-the-End-Times-January-2016.pdf

about the timing of the return of Jesus (regardless of what that timing turns out to be)! Let me state that again, and let it sink in:

> ***By definition*, the majority of Protestant pastors are mistaken about the timing of the Rapture.**

I am not saying you shouldn't trust your pastor, but on *this* issue, statistically there is a greater than 60% chance that he is mistaken!

The Lifeway Research results are consolidated in the following graphic:

**Figure 1: Rapture Timing Theories**

| Rapture Theory | Church Endures the Tribulation | Percentage | Require Preparation |
|---|---|---|---|
| Pretribulation | No | 36% | No |
| Rapture not Literal | - | 26% | - |
| Post-tribulation | Yes | 18% | Yes |
| Prewrath | Yes | 4% | Yes |
| Mid-tribulation | Yes | 4% | Yes |

Although this graphic appears complex, the results are actually quite simple to interpret. There are only two "camps" or divisions among the rapture theories:

- those that believe the church will endure a least a portion of the Tribulation and will require preparation.
- those that don't believe this.

Although there are nuanced differences between the post-tribulation, prewrath, and mid-tribulation rapture theories, they can be grouped together for simplicity because they share the common belief that the church will face at least a portion of the Tribulation. In this way, we have broken the Rapture discussion down into its most basic question:

> **"Will the church face The Tribulation and need to prepare?" All other issues are secondary.**

In order to answer this question, we will contrast two of the five theories: the pretribulation rapture theory and the prewrath rapture theory*. The first theory answers our primary question with the response, "No, the church will not face the Tribulation." The second theory answers, "Yes, it will."

(*Please note: the reason that the prewrath theory was chosen to represent those theories [the post-tribulation, prewrath, and mid-tribulation theories] answering "yes" to the primary question will become apparent as we proceed throughout the rest of the book.)

So out of a myriad of Rapture theories, we have simplified the discussion to a binary choice. It is one or the other. The pretribulation rapture theory asserts that Christians will be rescued prior to the Tribulation. The prewrath rapture theory asserts Christians will be rescued after having endured the Great Tribulation. Let's spend a moment or so looking at simplified explanations of both theories.

### THE PRETRIBULATION RAPTURE THEORY

Both theories anticipate a rescue. This rescue is based on a verse from 1 Thessalonians:

14

Wait for His Son from heaven, whom He raised from the dead, that is Jesus, who *rescues us from the wrath to come* (1 Thess. 1:10 NASB, emphasis mine)

As we stated at the outset of this chapter, when Jesus returns he will punish the unrepentant and wicked of this world in his "wrath" or anger. But, God has promised in 1 Thess. 1:10 (and other verses) that Jesus will rescue Christians from this punishment before the Wrath of God is poured out. That rescue will take place at the Rapture. After this rescue into the presence of Jesus, this scenario suggests that Christians return with him to heaven where they will be safe while God's Wrath is poured out upon the earth.

The pretribulation rapture theory assumes the entire Tribulation period is the Wrath of God. Therefore, in order for God to save Christians from it, the Rapture must occur *before* the Tribulation begins. This theory is depicted in the graphic below:

**Figure 2: Pretribulation Rapture Model**

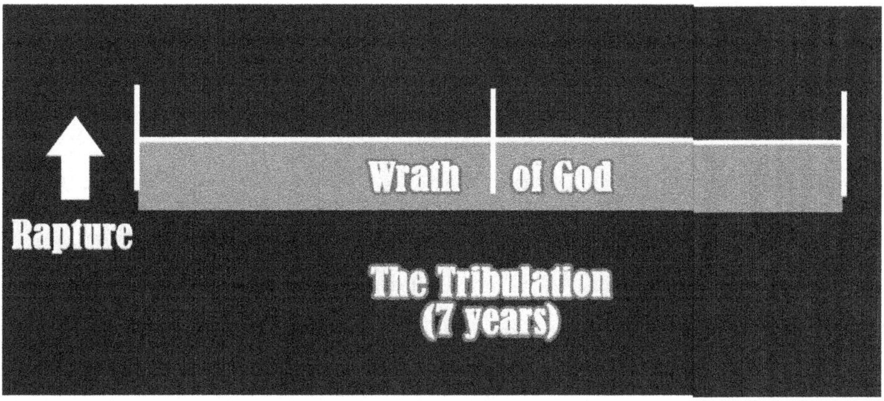

## THE PREWRATH RAPTURE THEORY

The prewrath theory makes a different assumption about when the Wrath of God begins. It assumes the wrath occurs *after* the Great Tribulation, towards the end of the 7-year period. Therefore, in order for God to save Christians from his punishment of the wicked, the Rapture must come *after* the Great Tribulation, yet before God's Wrath. So the Rapture is "prewrath" or before the Wrath of God. This theory is depicted in the following graphic:

**Figure 3: Prewrath Rapture Model**

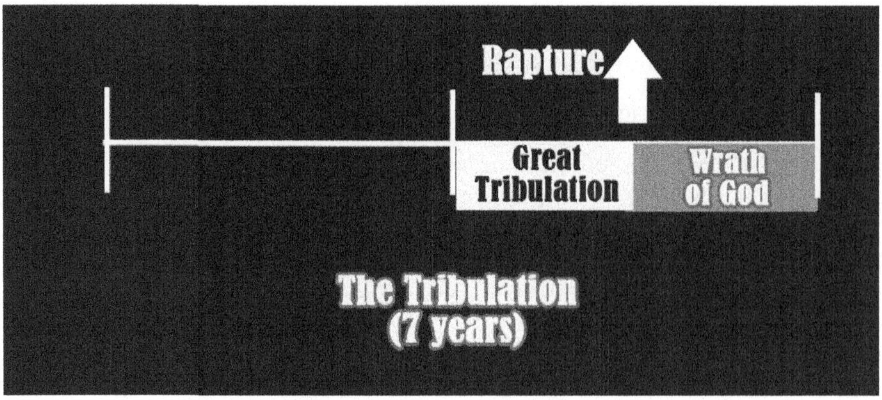

One simple change — the initiation point of God's Wrath — makes an enormous difference in impact. In the Pretrib. Rapture Model, the righteous escape the entire Tribulation period, but in the Prewrath Rapture Model, they don't, and would therefore need to prepare for this challenging time. Obviously, all Christians must know which model is correct . . . and which one is mistaken. That is the purpose of this book.

In the Part Two, we will systematically examine each of the three defining questions and solve the Rapture Puzzle.

# PART TWO:

## THREE DEFINING QUESTIONS

# Chapter Three

# WHY THESE THREE QUESTIONS?

*The Main Thing is to keep the Main Thing the main thing –*
*Rockwell Dillaman*

The quote above is from Pastor Rock Dillaman who baptized me in 1995 and also taught me many, many important spiritual lessons. None may have been more poignant than this gem about priorities. Keep the main thing the main thing. Focus on what is most important.

That is the key to simplicity, and frankly, it's the theme of this book. These three defining questions were not chosen because they are the most "exciting" or the most "controversial" or the most "popular." In fact, the first two questions are rarely discussed. However, if we answer them, we will know the timing of the Rapture with certainty. That is our goal.

## THE THREE DEFINING QUESTIONS

The Rapture Puzzle can be solved by answering three questions, the primary defining questions. Based on our discussion about God's Wrath in the previous chapter, you can probably anticipate the first one.

### 1. When does the Wrath of God Begin?

If we are able to discern with accuracy the point at which God's Wrath begins, we will be able to ascertain the point Jesus will rescue his faithful because his rescue is predicated on delivering Christians from that wrath.

19

2. **Is the passage in Matt. 24:29-31 depicting the physical return of Jesus to the earth to fight Armageddon or the Rapture?**

   The event depicted in Matt. 24:29-31 comes *after* great tribulation. If prewrath rapture theory is correct and it depicts the Rapture, there is no pretribulation rapture. If that theory is wrong and it's the physical Second Coming, there is no prewrath rapture. This is clearly a defining question.

3. **Can the Rapture occur at any time; is it "imminent?"**

   A prewrath Rapture must, by definition, occur after certain prophesied events take place found in Matt. 24. If the Rapture can occur at any time without the need for prophesied events to take place first, the Rapture will likely be pretribulational. Conversely, if prophesied events must take place before the Rapture, it cannot be pretribulational. Again, this is a defining question.

## WHY NOT LOOK AT OTHER "PROOFS?"

So why were these questions chosen and not one of hundreds of other questions? As we stated in chapter one, these were chosen because they definitely prove Rapture timing, and most of the other popular "Rapture proofs" do not. These other proofs may seem to demonstrate Rapture timing, but when closely examined they don't. And as we stated in that chapter, those other passages were never *intended* to prove Rapture timing! We will concentrate on those areas that *were intended* to edify the Body of Christ on this issue — a novel concept!

Let's look a few examples of these "rabbit hole" proofs that actually prove nothing about Rapture timing. For instance, why didn't we choose to discuss God's keeping Christians from the hour of testing?

> Because you have kept the word of My perseverance, I also
> will keep you from the hour of testing, that hour which is
> about to come upon the whole world, to test those who dwell
> on the earth. (Rev. 3:10 NASB)

This passage alludes to the Rapture, but it doesn't give us any indication of timing. You see, the followers of both the pretribulation rapture *and* the prewrath rapture believe God will keep the righteous from the hour of testing. One camp believes the hour is the entire Tribulation, the other believes it is the Wrath of God. So this isn't a defining question. It's sort of a draw.

Others might ask why this book didn't ask, "Why doesn't Revelation mention the word "church" (the Greek word *ekklesia*) between chapters 3 to 19?" as one of its three key questions. In Revelation, the word "church" never refers to the collective body of those who have placed their faith in Jesus. Revelation only uses *ekklesia* to refer to the proper name of the seven churches in Rev. 2 and 3 (Church of Ephesus, Church of Smyrna, etc.) or those seven churches collectively. In Revelation, the word "church" doesn't mean what many want it to mean; it doesn't mean "the" church. It refers to "a" specific church or "seven" specific churches. Therefore, this isn't a defining issue either. It neither proves nor disproves any theory. It is a "rabbit hole" leading nowhere.

Still others might ask why this book didn't choose a question about the restrainer of 2 Thess. 2? The reason is the Bible never identifies the restrainer. Some surmise it is the Holy Spirit and that he is taken out of the way at the Rapture. Others surmise it is the restraining influence of the church which is also removed at the Rapture. Others believe it is Michael the Archangel. But, the brightest pretribulation and prewrath scholars all admit that these theories are just supposition on the part of some believers. The identity of the restrainer and *why* he stops restraining the Antichrist isn't mentioned in the Scriptures. We just don't know. It, like so many other rapture "proofs," is a "rabbit hole." One that distracts us from our primary mission to answer the question, "Will the church face the Tribulation and does it need to prepare for it?"

This book chose the three defining questions because they definitely answer the question about Rapture timing in a simple, clear manner. It is obvious to me that they were the sections of Scripture intended for us to use to determine Rapture timing. So this book chose them to clear away the clutter of a hundred "rabbit holes" that lead nowhere.

In the next chapter, we'll begin to examine the first of the questions.

# Chapter Four

# WHEN DOES THE WRATH OF GOD BEGIN?

*. . . Wait for His Son from heaven, whom He raised from the*
*dead, that is Jesus, who rescues us from the wrath to come.*
*(1 Thess. 1:10 NASB)*

In chapter two, we determined that Jesus will rescue or rapture his church prior to the wrath to come, and that the entire Rapture Puzzle centers on when that wrath begins. Is the entire Tribulation period the Wrath of God (implying a pretribulation rapture) or does the Wrath of God begin after the Great Tribulation (implying a prewrath rapture)? The very definitions the two rapture theories depend on this primary defining question: "When does the Wrath of God Begin?"

Beginnings are sometimes very easy to pinpoint, and sometimes they are very hard to nail down to a specific day or time. For instance, when did the United States enter World War II? Although this horrible war began in Europe in 1939, and although President Franklin Roosevelt feverishly prepared the USA for war in 1939 - 1941, and although the Japanese attacked Pearl Harbor on Dec. 7, 1941, and although the President gave a stirring speech to the nation on the next day (Dec. 8, 1941), the United States did not formally enter the war until all but one member of Congress passed a resolution later on that same day. A very specific written Act of Congress declared and initiated the USA's involvement in the war.

Now to many this is a confusing point. On Dec. 7, 1941, American sailors were actively fighting against Japanese pilots on the Island of Hawaii.

But this was an engagement, it wasn't war. By law, the United States isn't at war with another nation until Congress declares it is at war.

In the same way, the Wrath of God does not begin until God's Word says it begins. There may be a multitude of preliminary events prior to God's Wrath, but it only makes sense that something this important will be marked by a "decree" in the Scriptures. And there is such a Scripture:

> For the great day of *their (the Father, Son, and Holy Spirit's)* ***wrath has come***, and who is able to stand? (Rev. 6:17 NASB, clarification and emphasis mine)

This is simple to understand. It may be unpopular, but it's strikingly clear and simple. This verse states that on a specific "great day," the wrath of the Father, Son, and Holy Spirit will begin. And because this verse so unambiguously defines the beginning of the Wrath of God, it has been attacked. Before we describe these attacks on God's Word, let's unpack the meaning and timing of this primary verse.

## THE MEANING OF REV. 6:17

This verse, which may be the "one verse" that all the radio talk shows are asking about, is found in the sixth chapter of Revelation. In that chapter, Jesus opens a great scroll in heaven bound with seven seals. Throughout history, important documents have been sealed shut with wax or clay seals which prevent the document from being tampered with. In this same way, God's Word describes this most important of all documents as being sealed until the Holy Son of God removes the seals and opens it.

After Jesus removes the sixth of seven seals, the sun and moon are darkened, the stars fall to the earth, the sky rolls up like a scroll, and a great earthquake moves the mountains and islands. It is after these earth-shaking events (literally earth-shaking) that we read the reaction of those on the earth:

> Then the kings of the earth and the great men and the
> commanders and the rich and the strong and every slave and
> free man hid themselves in the caves and among the rocks of
> the mountains. (Rev. 6:15 NASB)

This is history written in advance. A day is coming when everyone on earth will look to hide themselves in the rocks and the caves. It will be a day like no other. It will be an unmistakable day. Why are they hiding? Is it to protect themselves from the falling stars?

> And they said to the mountains and to the rocks, "Fall on us
> and hide us from *the presence (literally: face) of Him who sits*
> *on the throne*, and from the wrath of the Lamb.
> (Rev. 6:17 NASB, clarification and emphasis mine)

No! They are asking to be hidden from the face of God! No living person can see the Father, so this is God, the Son, sitting upon his throne, and they are asking to be hidden from Him—and his *wrath*. This event is occurring in Rev. 6, long before Jesus rides a white horse and returns to fight Armageddon. Therefore, Jesus is visible to every person on earth before his final physical return; before all the Trumpets sound and before all the Bowls are poured out.

Additionally, all the inhabitants of the earth are asking to be hidden from Jesus's wrath. And it is into this context that our "one verse" appears.

For the great day of *their wrath has come*, and who is able to stand? (Rev. 6:17 NASB, emphasis mine)

Now that we appreciate the context, let's unpack this verse; and God has packed amazing content into these few words.

First, notice that it is the "great day of their wrath" that has come or just begun. The verse does not say that God's wrath has come just yet, only that the day his wrath will be poured out has come. This is an important nuance of understanding. The Wrath of God can (and will be) poured out later that same 24-hour day.

Second, notice the wrath is not just of Jesus as mentioned in the previous verse, but it the great day of *their* wrath. God's Word makes this very important distinction that it is the Wrath of the triune God; that it is the eschatological, final Wrath of God mentioned by the prophets, not simply a minor wrath of the Son alone. Again, this is a key nuance of understanding.

Then third, it is a "great day" of wrath; it is the Great and Terrible Day of the Lord as mentioned in the prophets. The Old Testament mentions several "Days of the Lord" throughout the history of Israel, but there is only one final, eschatological, "Great and Terrible Day of the Lord." God's Word wants us to know clearly and unambiguously that this is it!

And finally, the verse tells us that the Wrath of God "has come." Much has been made of this little verb. It is found in the aorist tense, which in the Greek is a "timeless" tense. In other words, it must rely on context for its timing. Dr. David L. Mathewson of Denver Seminary demonstrates that the aorist can have up to eight different tense distinctions depending on context[2]. One of these uses is the *ingressive* which marks the beginning of an action.

---

[2] Mathewson, David and Emig, Elodie, *Intermediate Greek Grammar*, (Baker Academic, Grand Rapids, 2016), pp. 119-125.

And this is the clear meaning in Rev. 6:17. No one asks to be hidden under rocks from something that started years earlier. "Fall on us and hide us because the great day of their wrath *started six years ago*." This is a nonsense statement that no one would make. People only ask to be hidden from what they perceive to be a present danger and at its inception!

Yet, because the Greek aorist (a tense not found in English) can also refer to past actions (among its eight tense distinctions), many highly respected pretribulationalists try to obscure the impact of Rev. 6:17 by claiming this other meaning of aorist in this usage. But, as can be plainly seen, the context precludes it. And, of course, all major English translations (NASB, ESV, NKJV, and NIV) acknowledge this fact and correctly translate the verb as "has come" not "had come."

In conclusion, there is zero doubt that the Great Day of the Lord, the Wrath of God, begins after Jesus opens the sixth seal. This is indisputable based on Scripture. And it is SIMPLE, easy to understand, . . . and unpopular.

## The Timing of Rev. 6:17

Rev. 6:17 is unpopular because once we understand the timing of the sixth seal and the Great and Terrible Day of the Lord, it solves the Rapture puzzle, which makes the majority of people initially unhappy.

The sixth seal of Revelation is marked by earth-shattering events: the darkening of the sun and moon, stars falling to earth, the sky being rolled up as a scroll, and an earthquake that moves mountains and islands. This event is found in a number of other passages in Scripture. It is the sign that portends the soon return of Jesus. In the Gospel of Matthew, we are given the *timing* of this event as well:

But immediately *after the tribulation* of those days (after the

Great Tribulation) the sun will be darkened, and the moon

will not give its light, and the stars will fall from the sky, and

the powers of the heavens will be shaken. (Matt. 24:29

NASB, clarification and emphasis mine)

This event, the sixth seal, happens after the "tribulation of those days" which

Jesus had just specified was the Great Tribulation. The Wrath of God doesn't

happen before the Tribulation (pretribulational), at the middle of the

Tribulation (mid-tribulational), or at the very end of the Tribulation (post-

tribulational). This is what makes this teaching initially unpopular. It goes

against most popular Rapture positions.

### INTERPRETING THE WORD OF GOD

Because this teaching is unpopular, it has been attacked. You may have heard

that the Wrath of God begins with the first seal — not after the sixth seal. This

is a very common teaching. In order to state this, however, one must be

willing to deny what God's Word has clearly stated in Rev. 6:17, that the great

day of our triune God's Wrath begins or "has come" after the sixth seal.

Now, how is it that many learned and righteous men should make this

mistake? Is it intentional? I sincerely doubt it. You see elsewhere in Rev. 6

there are passages that to them *imply* that God's Wrath starts earlier. And

since that fits with their preferred pretribulation rapture theory, they accept it.

But "implying" is not the same as clearly stating something. Remember, Rev.

6:17 clearly states the correct timing. Let's explore their theory see why it is

mistaken.

Dr. Mark Hitchcock, a renowned pretribulation rapture scholar,

summarizes this concept:

The seal judgments which are opened at the beginning of the tribulation are brought forth not by man or Satan, but by the Lamb Himself, the Lord Jesus Christ (Rev. 6:1). They are messianic judgments. Jesus opens the seals and an angel calls each of the four horsemen to ride across the earth in judgment.[3]

—Dr. Mark Hitchcock

Dr. Hitchcock is an attorney, the author of twenty books, a senior pastor, and adjunct faculty for the Dallas Theological Seminary. The first thing to notice about his statement is that unlike Rev. 6:17, Dr. Hitchcock's assessment is not based on an *explicit* statement in the Word of when the Wrath of God begins. His position is an assumption based on the events occurring in Rev. 6:1-2.

This lack of an explicit reference to God's Wrath is very important to understand. Just like our analogy about the USA's involvement in WWII earlier in this chapter, events may *appear* to indicate war had begun, when in reality, the legal involvement of the USA in the war didn't happen until years later on Dec. 8, 1941. We need to be very careful about stating something is God's Wrath without God *telling us in his Word* that it is his Wrath.

The verse which contains Hitchcock's assumptions follows:

Then I saw when the Lamb broke one of the seven seals, and I heard one of the four living creatures saying as with a voice of thunder, "Come." I looked, and behold, a white horse, and he who sat on it had a bow; and a crown was given to him, and he went out conquering and to conquer. (Rev. 6:1-2 NASB)

---

[3] "An Overview of Pre-Tribulational Arguments," Pre-Trib. Research Center, last modified unknown, accessed May 4, 2016, http://www.pre-trib.org/articles/view/an-overview-of-pretribulatonal-arguments

As we continue to consider Dr. Hitchcock's position (which is the primary position of the pretribulation rapture theory), we see that three similar events occur in conjunction with each of the first four seals: First, Jesus opens the seal, then second, one of the living creatures says, "Come," and finally a horse and rider come forth. This can be interpreted two ways:

- When the living creatures say "Come," they could be **commanding** the horsemen to come forth. This would indicate that they were relaying Jesus's command, and that Jesus himself was causing or ordering the events that follow the seals.

- When the living creatures say "Come," they could also simply be giving the horsemen **permission** to come forth. This would be similar to the way God gave Satan permission to test Job in Job 1-2. In this second scenario, it would be Satan and the Antichrist causing the events after each seal, but God is permitting them to do so.

Both scenarios are possible given the wording of Rev. 6, so we need to rely on context to determine if Dr. Hitchcock is correct or incorrect in his interpretation.

### ARE THE SEAL EVENTS CONSISTENT WITH GOD'S WRATH?

First, we can look at the events taking place after each seal to see if it is consistent with the Wrath of God, which is God's *punishment* on the ungodly. I contend that neither the first seal, the fourth seal, nor the fifth seal conform to that definition.

Most major eschatology teachers (both pretribulational and prewrath) assert that the events in Matt. 24 are parallel to the events in Rev. 6. These teachers include stalwarts of the pretrib. position such as Dr. Thomas Ice[4], Dr. John Walvoord, and Dr. Hitchcock himself[5]. This position asserts that the first seal is parallel to Matt. 24:4-5, which concerns deception by false prophets and false messiahs:

> And Jesus answered and said to them, "See to it that no one *misleads* you. For many will come in My name, saying, 'I am the Christ,' and will *mislead* many. (Matt. 24:4-5 NASB, emphasis mine)

The *misleading* and tempting to sin accomplished by the false prophets and messiahs are **not** things associated with God. "Let no one say when he is tempted, 'I am being tempted by God'; for God cannot be tempted by evil, and He Himself does not tempt anyone" (Jam. 1:13 NASB). So the first seal is completely inconsistent with being a work of God.

Second, the fourth seal is also inconsistent with the Wrath of God. The last portion of the description of this seal mentions three forms of killing. These forms of killing are also found in the Old Testament and associated there with God's Wrath. Compare this, however, to the fourth seal:

> For thus says the Lord GOD, "How much more when I send *(command)* My four severe judgments against Jerusalem:

---

[4] "Rapture Debate between Alan Kurschner (Pre-Wrath) and Thomas Ice (Pre-Trib.)," Eschatos Ministries, last modified September 27, 2015, accessed April 6, 2016, http://www.alankurschner.com/2015/09/27/rapture-debate-between-alan-kurschner-prewrath-and-thomas-ice-pretrib/ TIME: 1:17:15.

[5] John Walvoord, Mark Hitchcock, and Phillip Rawley, *Revelation*, (Moody Publishers, Chicago, 2011), Chapter 6

> sword, famine, wild beasts and plague to cut off man and
> beast from it! (Ezek. 14:21 NASB, clarification mine)

> Authority was given to them *(permission)* over a fourth of the
> earth, to kill with sword and with famine and with pestilence
> and by (Gk: *hypo* meaning under the authority of) the wild
> beasts of the earth. (Rev. 6:8 NASB, clarification mine)

Although these statements from the Old and New Testaments are similar, they are not the same. In the historic statement in Ezekiel, it is God who **commanded** the plagues. In the future fourth seal, God grants **permission** or authority for the killing; he doesn't command it. Also, in the statement about the fourth seal, it is the beasts (the Antichrist and False Prophet) who are actually supervising the killing. It is under their authority. This is entirely consistent with our proposed scenario that the events after the first four seals represent God granting **permission** to the horsemen to perform their deeds, not God **commanding** those events. There is an enormous difference between the two.

Additionally, and *most importantly*, in the case of both the fourth and fifth seal, the primary targets of the killing are those who have chosen to testify about Jesus and become martyrs. Obviously, God's Wrath is not poured out on the faithful! **Frankly, this is an insurmountable problem for the pretrib. position**. The Great Tribulation is a time when believers are slaughtered for being faithful and testifying about Jesus. In contrast, the unrepentant have food provided under the Mark of the Beast and have their lives spared because they worship the Antichrist. This is the polar opposite of God's Wrath; it is punishment of the righteous and reward of the wicked. Anyone who states the Great Tribulation is part of God's Wrath needs to

32

carefully examine their motivations for making such a statement which is contrary to the nature of God.

### EYE-WITNESS STATEMENTS

In addition to the nature of events during the seals that preclude them from being God's Wrath, God has also placed three *eye-witness* statements within his Holy Word that are explicit testimony that the first five seals are not part of the Wrath of God. The first statement, of course, is Rev. 6:17 as we have discussed earlier in this chapter. In this statement, all the inhabitants of the earth testify as to the timing of the initiation of the Great and Terrible Day of the Lord's Wrath.

The second group of eye-witnesses speak out after the opening of the fifth seal. They are martyrs who died because of their testimony and because of the Word of God. Their statement is quite telling:

> They cried out with a loud voice, saying, "How long, O Lord,
> holy and true, will You *refrain from judging and avenging*
> our blood on those who dwell on the earth?"
> (Rev. 6:10 NASB, emphasis mine)

Our righteous God would never punish and avenge without judging first. This declaration by these eye-witnesses clearly states that after the opening of the fifth seal, God still had not *begun* to judge or punish. This precludes all five of the first seals from being God's Wrath.

Finally, a third witness cries out from the pages of the Old Testament. The prophet Joel clearly testifies that the Great and Terrible Day of the Lord (God's Wrath) follows the sixth seal events:

The sun will be turned into darkness and the moon into blood *before* the great and awesome day of the LORD comes. (Joel 2:31 NASB, emphasis mine)

All three eye-witness statements are completely consistent with the position that we have presented in this chapter that the day of God's Wrath begins after the opening of the sixth seal and **not** at the beginning of the Tribulation.

The pretrib. contention that the Wrath of God begins with the opening of the first seal initially seems plausible. However, the events that follow the seals and the eye-witness testimonies that God has strategically placed in Scripture absolutely preclude that contention. God's Wrath undoubtedly begins after the sixth seal which occurs after the Great Tribulation, uniquely consistent with a prewrath rapture.

The only rational conclusion to this analysis is that there is no pretribulation rapture and that the rapture will be prewrath.

## "RABBIT HOLES"

It is at this point that most readers who favor a pretribulation rapture position begin to search for a "rabbit hole" by saying, "yes, but what about this other proof or that other proof." But before you resort to that, please consider that God's Word is entirely consistent and cannot contradict itself. We have just proved that the timing of the Wrath of God (the justification for all rapture positions) precludes a pretribulation rapture. So instead of continuing to look for support for that theory which has already been disproven, consider why those other rapture proofs you favor *do not* prove the pretribulation rapture either. Be transformed by the renewing of your mind by the Word of God.

However, I realize that is difficult. For that reason, let's examine one of the primary "rabbit holes" that one is tempted to go down at this point: "My

Jesus would never subject us to the Great Tribulation. The Tribulation must be the Wrath of God." Pastor Billy Crone of "Get A Life Ministries" has this to say about being present in the seven-year tribulation:

> That's not good news, that's not a blessed hope, that's bad news.
> —Pastor Billy Crone[6]

Pastor Crone is obviously referring to Titus 2:13: "Looking for the blessed hope and the appearing of the glory of our great God and Savior, Christ Jesus." His statement implies that for the appearing of Jesus to truly be a blessed hope or good news, Christians will need to avoid the Great Tribulation, admittedly the "greatest" time of tribulation since the creation. This statement by Pastor Crone, which echoes the sentiments of nearly all pretribulation rapture theorists, however, overlooks several great truths.

First, our "hope" is not in earthly comfort, safety, or possessions. **Our hope is in Jesus**, and his glorious return is a blessed hope no matter what struggles or persecution intervenes between now and then. Even enduring the great tribulation will not lessen our blessed hope by even the slightest amount.

Second, God did not promise to insulate us from suffering or persecution (tribulation). In fact, he promised us that in this world, we *will* endure tribulation (John. 16:33). He even further stated that "*Blessed* are those who have been persecuted for the sake of righteousness" (Matt. 5:10 NASB).

---

[6] "When Will the Believing be Leaving?" *Understanding the Times with Jan Markel*, last modified Jan. 14, 2017, accessed June 7, 2017, http://www.oneplace.com/ministries/understanding-the-times/custom-player

**Many are currently enduring tribulation equal to what will occur in the Great Tribulation at the hands of Islamic jihadists. Do these believers not have a blessed hope because they endure persecution, torture, and death?**

Third, the term "great tribulation" is misconstrued. The Greek word translated "great" in Matthew 24:21 is *megas*, which means "large or widespread." It does not mean "worse or more painful." By using this term, Jesus was telling us that the tribulation will be more widespread than ever before. It is hard to imagine worse persecution than what some believers are currently enduring in the Middle East, but it is easy to imagine that type of persecution being more widespread.

This pretribulation rapture belief that Christians should expect to be kept away from persecution is in direct contrast with the teachings of the New Testament that repeatedly tell us to *expect* to suffer for the cause of Christ. If you have believed this errant teaching, please consider the example of Jesus and the disciples who, with one exception, died a martyr's death. Should we aspire to be different from them or emulate them?

**Conclusion**

I know this concept of proving the Rapture with one proof may be difficult for you, but that is the beauty of simplicity. If we are able to categorically disprove a rapture theory (the pretribulation rapture) using one proof, it is disproven using every proof because God's Word is consistent. Remember, not every passage about the return of Jesus was intended to give us information about its timing. Rev. 6, however, certainly was. That is why it is of critical importance in understanding this issue.

## Chapter Five

# IS MATT. 24:31 THE SECOND COMING OR THE RAPTURE?

*And He will send forth His angels with a great trumpet and they*
*will gather together His elect from the four winds, from one end*
*of the sky to the other. (Matt. 24:31 NASB)*

To most, the title of this chapter must seem almost scandalous. Ninety-six percent of Christians (or more) consider Matt. 24:31 to be the physical Second Coming of Jesus when he returns to fight Armageddon. Most are probably wondering if I have lost my sanity. "How can it be anything but the physical Second Coming?" they chuckle. If it is the Rapture as I contend, however, this verse will go down as the greatest case of Scriptural mistaken identity in history!

Adolf Beck of London is probably the most famous criminal case of mistaken identity. One day as he innocently walked down the street, a woman accused him of defrauding her of a wristwatch and rings. Beck happened to slightly resemble the actual swindler, John Smith, who was wanted for numerous crimes. The police arrested Beck and placed him in line-ups for that crime and other crimes as well. Because Beck was the only gray-haired, mustachioed man in the line-ups, he was identified as the criminal in multiple crimes. At his trial, Beck was able to prove he was not Smith. Beck's evidence was undeniable. Smith was circumcised, and Beck was not, and Beck was able to prove he was out of the country at the time of many of the crimes. Yet incredibly, despite overwhelming evidence in his favor, Beck was found guilty and served five years in prison.

Upon his release, he was again arrested for a crime committed by a distinguished, grey-haired gentleman! Except this time, the witness was uncertain it was Beck. But the policeman arrested him anyway, sure the perpetrator was Beck based on his previous convictions. Eventually the actual swindler was found and arrested, but not until after Beck had served two prison terms.

Although Beck's misidentification was tragic, if Matt. 24:31 has been misidentified, hundreds of millions of Christians may be hoodwinked into believing in a pretribulation rapture that will not happen—even more tragic.

### TWO EVENTS — BUT THREE PASSAGES

In chapter two, we discussed how both the pretribulation rapture theory and the prewrath rapture theory anticipate that Jesus will rescue the righteous prior to the Wrath (or punishment) of God. Pretribulation followers believe this will occur prior to the Tribulation, prewrath followers believe this will occur after the Great Tribulation, but both groups believe this rescue event happens *before* the end of the seven-year Tribulation.

At the end of the Tribulation, a second event occurs which we will term the physical Second Coming. At this time, Jesus will mount a white horse and return with all the believers he raptured into heaven to fight the final battle against evil: Armageddon. These two events are depicted in the following graphic:

## Figure 4: Rapture and Second Coming

Nearly all Christians believe that the first event, the Rapture, is depicted in Scripture by the following familiar passage in 1 Thess. as we discussed in chapter two.

> For the Lord Himself will descend from heaven with a shout, with the voice of the archangel and with the trumpet of God, and the dead in Christ will rise first. Then we who are alive and remain will be caught up together with them in the clouds to meet the Lord in the air, and so we shall always be with the Lord. (1 Thess. 4:16-17 NASB)

In the same way, nearly all Christians also believe that the second event, the physical Second Coming, is depicted in Scripture by this equally familiar passage in Rev. 19.

> I saw heaven opened, and behold, a white horse, and He who sat on it is called Faithful and True, and in righteousness He judges and wages war. His eyes are a flame of fire, and on his

39

head are many diadems; and he has a name written on Him
which no one knows except himself. He is clothed with a robe
dipped in blood, and his name is called The Word of God.
And the armies which are in heaven, clothed in fine linen,
white and clean, were following Him on white horses. From
His mouth comes a sharp sword, so that with it He may strike
down the nations, and He will rule them with a rod of iron;
and He treads the wine press of the fierce wrath of God, the
Almighty. And on His robe and on His thigh, He has a name
written, "King of kings, and Lord of lords." (Rev. 19:11-16
NASB)

If we represent each of these passages with icons, we can add them to the
graphic we developed. The resulting graphic is pictured below.

## Figure 5: Rapture and Second Coming Passages

There is a third great "return of Jesus" passage in scripture, however. Actually, several versions of this passage are found in the gospel accounts (Matt. 24:29-31, Mark 13:26-27, Luke 21:25-27). The account in Matthew is the most well-known:

> But immediately after the tribulation of those days the sun
> will be darkened, and the moon will not give its light, and the
> stars will fall from the sky, and the powers of the heavens will
> be shaken. And then the sign of the Son of Man will appear in
> the sky, and then all the tribes of the earth will mourn, and
> they will see the Son of Man coming on the clouds of the sky
> with power and great glory. And he will send forth His angels
> with a great trumpet and they will gather together His elect
> from the four winds, from one end of the sky to the other.
> (Matt. 24:29-31 NASB)

Now historically, this passage has been considered the same event as Rev. 19:11-16 by pretribulation rapture theorists, post-tribulation rapture theorists, and mid-tribulation rapture theorists. The reason that these passages have been considered the same event is *not* based on sound biblical interpretation, but rather because scholars were at a loss for what else the event in Matt. 24 could be! If it isn't the physical Second Coming, what is it?

However, after the prewrath rapture theory was first articulated by Robert Van Kampen and Marvin Rosenthal in the 1990's, a second option became apparent. Perhaps it's the rapture, perhaps it's the prewrath rapture.

If we try to add an icon on our graphic for Matt. 24:29-31, initially we are at a loss for where to position it. The pretribulation rapture theorists want to position it with Rev. 19:11-16 as a physical Second Coming passage and the prewrath rapture theorists want to position it as a rapture passage along with 1 Thess. 4:16-17.

## Figure 6: Where Does Matt. 24 Belong?

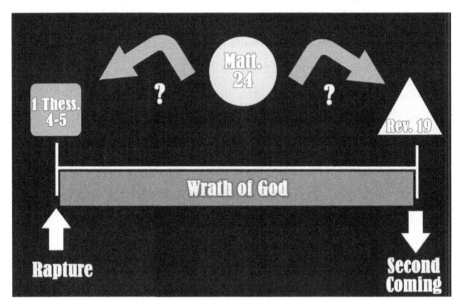

### ONE OF THESE THINGS IS NOT LIKE THE OTHERS

This difference of opinion gives us our second scriptural truth to solve the rapture puzzle. If we can prove that Matt. 24:29-31 is a rapture passage and not a physical Second Coming passage, we will have categorically disproven the pretribulation Rapture (and the post-tribulation and mid-tribulation rapture positions as well)!

This is a very simple concept. And in keeping with our theme of simplicity, we can play the children's game, "One of these things is not like the others" to determine which is which.

## Figure 7: One of these things is not like the others

This is a simple approach, but it is far from a childlike approach. It is sound biblical exegesis allowing Scripture to interpret Scripture. Matt. 24:29-31 will share features in common with whatever other "return of Jesus" passage depicts the same event. If it's the Rapture, it will share many common features with 1 Thess. 4:16-17. If it's the physical Second Coming, it will share common features with Rev. 19:11-16. And, as we will soon observe, Matt. 24:29-31 and its surrounding verses will exhibit features that absolutely *preclude* it from being the same as one of the other two passages!

The following graphic (continuing on the next page) depicts fifteen areas of comparison between the passages.

## Figure 8: Comparison between 1 Thess., Matt. 24, and Rev. 19

| Area of Comparison | 1 Thess. 4-5 | Matt. 24 | Rev. 19 |
|---|---|---|---|
| Called a "coming" | ☑ 4:15 | ☑ 24:27,37,39 | ☒ |
| Refers to a resurrection | ☑ 4:16 | ☑ 24:21 | ☒ |
| Likened to birth pains | ☑ 5:3 | ☑ 24:8 | ☒ |
| Sinners are referred to as "drunk" | ☑ 5:7 | ☑ 24:49 | ☒ |
| Presence of angels | ☑ 4:16 | ☑ 24:31 | ☒ |

| Area of Comparison | 1 Thess. 4-5 | Matt. 24 | Rev. 19 |
|---|---|---|---|
| Trumpet of God | ✓ 4:16 | ✓ 24:31 | ✗ |
| Jesus is specified as being in the clouds | ✓ 4:17 | ✓ 24:30 | ✗ |
| Jesus gathers the elect together | ✓ 4:17 | ✓ Mark 13:27 | ✗ |
| Direction of the gathering of righteous is up | ✓ 4:17 | ✓ Mark 13:27 | ✗ Elect descend with Jesus |
| Timing unknown | ✓ 5:1 | ✓ 24:36 | ✗ |
| Comes as a thief | ✓ 5:2, 4 | ✓ 24:43 | ✗ |
| Takes the unrepentant by surprise | ✓ 5:2 | ✓ 24:36-39 | ✗ Rev. 16:15 Satan/Antichrist aren't surprised |
| Followed by fiery judgment | | ✓ Reference to Rev. 8:7 | ✗ No fire falls at Armageddon |
| The Trumpet and Bowl Judgments | | ✓ Trumpets and Bowls are not mentioned | ✗ Must occur after the Trumpets and 6 of the Bowls |
| Jesus's Robes | | ✓ Consistent with Jesus's robes being stained in Rev.19:15 | ✗ Jesus's robes were stained prior to Rev. 19:15 |

I'm sure the overwhelming result of this comparison is shocking. The first eleven comparisons are consistent between 1 Thess. and Matt. 24, and the final six comparisons absolutely prohibit Matt. 24 and Rev. 19 from being the same events.

Whatever Rapture timing theory you ascribed to prior to reading this book, I'm sure this comparison chart has caught your attention. Just as the scriptural truth about the Wrath of God in the previous chapter leads to only one conclusion — the prewrath rapture — in the same way, this scriptural truth also eliminates every other rapture timing theory. This is "Simplifying the Rapture." We don't need 147 proofs because each of these Scriptural proofs indicate that one and only one Rapture timing theory is possible.

In the following sections, we will unpack these areas of comparison shown in Figure 8, so you can understand the theology behind each one. Remember that Matt. 24:29-31 has to be referring to the Rapture or to the physical Second Coming; there are no other choices!

### CALLED A "COMING" OR *PAROUSIA*

A common compliant of post-tribulation rapture theorists is that they claim Jesus can't have more than one second "coming." They claim that scripture is clear that he has one and only one coming or parousia (the Greek word translated "coming"). I agree completely! What is shocking to most post-tribulation rapture followers, however, is that the passage in Rev. 19:11-16 is not a coming even though it is called the Second Coming in our Christian culture! In fact, the term "Second Coming" is not found in Scripture. In the Greek New Testament, Jesus's return is indicated by four different terms:

- *Erchomai*, which is "come." It is a generic word and is found 637 times in the New Testament. A small number of these uses refer to Jesus's return in glory.
- *Apokaluptó*, which means "uncovering or revealing." Jesus can only be revealed to the world one time. This is a singular event.

45

- *Epiphaneia*, which means "appearing" or more specifically the "appearing of a god."
- *Parousia*, is a semi-technical term, which in the Middle East of Jesus's day meant "visit of a royal dignitary or official."

And Rev. 19:11-16 isn't called by any of these terms. It isn't a coming or revealing or appearing or royal visit. Jesus had already "come" prior to that event. So even though our culture calls Rev. 19:11-16 the Second Coming, it really isn't. However, both 1 Thess. and Matt. 24 *are* termed the coming or the *parousia* or "royal visit."

> We who are alive and remain until *the coming (parousia)* of the Lord, will not precede those who have fallen asleep. (1 Thess. 4:15 NASB, emphasis mine)

> For just as the lightning comes from the east and flashes even to the west, so will *the coming (parousia)* of the Son of Man be. (Matt. 24:27 NASB, emphasis mine)

This is an incredibly important argument. Not only is the term *parousia* used in both passages, but the term is singular and preceded by the definitive article, "the." They are both "the" *parousia* or coming of Jesus; the one and only "coming."

> **If 1 Thess. 4-5 and Matt. 24 are both the one and only coming of Jesus, they are the same event.**

In and of itself, this point disproves the pretribulation rapture theory entirely. (The events in Matthew and 1 Thessalonians cannot simultaneously be the same thing and there be a pretrib. rapture because, as we have seen in the last chapter, the Rapture in Matt. 24:31 comes *after* Great Tribulation.)

## THE RESURRECTION

Both 1 Thessalonians and Matthew refer to the resurrection of dead believers, while Rev. 19 makes no mention of a Resurrection. This is also a definitive, but poorly understood, proof. The Resurrection is a key feature of the passage in 1 Thessalonians:

> For the Lord Himself will descend from heaven with a shout, with the voice of the archangel and with the trumpet of God, and *the dead in Christ will rise first*. (1 Thess. 4:16 NASB, emphasis mine)

However, most scholars miss that the Matthew passage also includes the Resurrection because it is found there by *reference* and not directly mentioned. Jesus warned his listeners that a Great Tribulation will come. His apostles would have recognized his warning as quote from the prophet Daniel:

> There will be a great tribulation, such as has not occurred since the beginning of the world until now, nor ever will. (Matt. 24:21 NASB)

> There will be a time of distress such as never occurred since there was a nation until that time. (Dan. 12:1 NASB)

By quoting Daniel, Jesus let them (and us) know that the "time of distress" mentioned in Daniel will be the Great Tribulation. However, Daniel's passage didn't stop at that point. He continued:

> And *at that time* your people, everyone who is found written in the book, will be rescued. *Many of those who sleep in the dust of the ground will awake*, these to everlasting life, but the others to disgrace and everlasting contempt. Those who have insight will shine brightly like the brightness of the expanse of heaven. (Dan. 12:1-3 NASB, emphasis mine)

The prophet Daniel mentioned three things that will happen "at that time" of unique distress (at the time of the Great Tribulation):

- everyone found written in "the book" (the book of life) will be rescued (raptured away from the Wrath of God),
- a Resurrection will occur, and
- those with insight will "shine." This final point is a likely reference to the righteous being transformed into resurrection bodies which will be like Christ's (1 Cor. 15:51-52).

By referencing Dan. 12:1, Jesus was letting his disciples (and us) know that the three other things that would happen "at that time" were also going to occur. So, although Jesus didn't mention the Resurrection directly in Matt. 24, his reference to Dan. 12 was a mention by reference. If the Great Tribulation was going to happen, the other things associated with the time of the Great Tribulation would happen as well, *including* the Resurrection.

Again, this is a definitive proof. If the Resurrection happens at the same time as the Great Tribulation (directly after it), there can be no pretribulation rapture. For this reason, many pretrib. theorists have suggested that the resurrection mentioned in Daniel is a separate resurrection only for righteous Old Testament Jews. By saying this, they imply that there will be more than one resurrection at the time of the Tribulation.

Unfortunately for their theory, Scripture precludes multiple resurrections at that time. In 1 Corinthians, Paul is very explicit about the order and timing of resurrections:

> For as in Adam all die, so also in Christ all will be made alive, but each in his own order: Christ the first fruits, after that *those who are Christ's at His coming (parousia), then comes the end* when he hands over the kingdom to the God and Father, when He has abolished all rule and all authority and power. For He must reign until He has put all His enemies under His feet. The last enemy that will be abolished is death. (1 Cor. 15:23-26 NASB, emphasis mine)

Paul informs us that a resurrection took place in the first century that included Jesus (and selected Old Testament saints). He calls this a "first fruits" resurrection. "First fruits" is a harvest term. Hebrew harvests were three-part: a "first fruits" harvest that were offered to God, the main-harvest, and finally a "gleanings" harvest to gather-in any grain the main-harvest missed. Paul informs us that the resurrections God has planned will mimic this three-part formula. The resurrection of Jesus and select Old Testament saints in the first century was the "first fruits" portion of the three-part resurrection harvest. He then tells us that the main-harvest resurrection will take place at Jesus's *parousia*, which we now know is pictured in 1 Thess. 4 and Matt. 24.

Then Paul makes an incredibly important statement: "Then comes the end." Paul is specific that this "end" is the point when Jesus abolishes death. We know that doesn't happen until after his 1000-year Millennial reign. So Paul has made it clear that there was one first fruits resurrection in the first century, a main-harvest resurrection at Jesus's *parousia* (at the Rapture) when all those who are "his" will be resurrected, and absolutely no other resurrections until the end of the Millennial Kingdom when the gleanings harvest will take place (Rev. 20:4-5). The importance of this statement cannot be overstated, so let me repeat it.

> **There will be no "extra" resurrections after the Rapture and before the end of the Millennial Kingdom.**

Some pretrib. theorists have suggested as many as seven resurrections! Obviously, this is inconsistent with the testimony of Scripture.

### OTHER CORRELATIONS BETWEEN MATTHEW AND 1 THESSALONIANS

The passages in Matt. and 1 Thess. have a myriad of other similarities that are not shared by Rev. 19. Both scripture passages are likened to the pain of a woman's childbirth (1 Thess. 5: 3, Matt. 24:8), both describe the sinful condition of the unrepentant as "drunkenness" (1 Thess. 5:7, Matt. 24:49), both include angels (1 Thess. 4:16, Matt. 24:31), both include the Trumpet of God (1 Thess. 4:16, Matt. 24:31), in both passages Jesus is in the clouds (1 Thess. 4:17, Matt. 24:30), both include an assembling together of the righteous up and into the air (1 Thess. 4:17, Mark 13:27).

**SURPRISE**

Not only are there numerous correlations between 1 Thessalonians and Matthew where the passage in Revelation is silent, but there are also some correlations between the first two passages that absolute preclude them from being the same as Rev. 19.

One of those areas of correlation is that Jesus's parousia will be a surprising event at an unknow time. Both 1 Thessalonians and Matthew clearly demonstrate this surprise element of Jesus's parousia:

> For you yourselves know full well that the day of the Lord will come just like a thief in the night. While they are saying, "Peace and safety!" then destruction will come upon them suddenly like labor pains upon a woman with child, and they will not escape. (1 Thess. 5:2 NASB)

> But of that day and hour no one knows, not even the angels of heaven, nor the Son, but the Father alone. For the coming of the Son of Man will be just like the days of Noah. For as in those days before the flood they were eating and drinking, marrying and giving in marriage, until the day that Noah entered the ark, and they did not understand until the flood came and took them all away (Matt. 24:36-39 NASB)

However, Rev. 19 and Armageddon will not take Satan and the Antichrist by surprise. In fact, they will gather the armies of the earth together to fight against Jesus *prior* to his Rev. 19 descent on a white horse.

For they are spirits of demons, performing signs, which go out to the kings of the whole world, to gather them together for the war of the great day of God, the Almighty. (Rev. 16:15 NASB)

So in 1 Thessalonians and Matthew, the unrepentant are not only surprised by Jesus's coming, but also by the sudden destruction that comes upon them. In contrast in Revelation, they are preparing for war against Jesus — they know he's comng. Although they probably don't expect to lose, the return of Jesus and the destruction that follows couldn't be considered surprising or sudden.

## THE TRUMPET AND BOWL JUDGMENTS

As we mentioned in chapter four, most biblical scholars believe that the events in Matt. 24 are the same and occur in the same order as those in Rev. 6. This one-for-one comparison is depicted in the graphic which continues on the following page:

### Figure 9: Comparison of Matt. 24 and Rev. 6

| Event | Matt. 24 | Rev. 6 |
|---|---|---|
| Deception by false messiahs | 24:4-5,23-26 | 6:1-2 |
| War and Chaos | 24:6-7 | 6:3-4 |
| Famine | 24:7 | 6:5-6 |
| Death and Abomination | 24:9,15-22 | 6:7-8 |
| Martyrdom and Testimony | 24:9-14 | 6:9-11 |
| Sun darkened | 24:29 | 6:12 |
| Moon darkened | 24:29 | 6:12 |
| Stars fall | 24:29 | 6:13 |

| Event | Matt. 24 | Rev. 6 |
|---|---|---|
| Heavens shaken | 24:29 | 6:14 |
| Tribes of the earth mourn | 24:30 | 6:15-17 |
| Jesus appears to all the inhabitants of earth | 24:30 | 6:16 |

If you've never been exposed to this teaching before, the amazing parallel nature of these passages (eleven events in exact order) is truly stunning. It is no wonder that a majority of teachers of eschatology have recognized this comparison as we detailed in the previous chapter.

The first insight we glean from the study of this graphic is that if Matt. 24 and Rev. 6 are the same set of events, then they cannot also be the same as a much later chapter, Rev. 19!

The second proof we can ascertain from this table is that if Matt. 24 and Rev. 6 are the same, then the Rapture in Matt. 24:31 is shortly followed (on the same day) by fiery judgment (Rev. 8:7, the first trumpet judgement). This makes the return of Jesus in Matt. 24 consistent with numerous passages in the Old and New Testaments which feature a fiery judgment upon the return of the Lord (Psalm 18, Isa. 9:18-19, Isa. 10:17-19, Isa. 30:27-33, Isa. 66:15–16, Ezek. 38:19–22, Jer. 25:15, 30–38, Hab. 3:5–6, Mal. 4:1-3, and others). However, Rev. 19:11-16 features *no fiery judgment at all*! This is a surprise to most if not all.

The third proof we can determine from this table is that the events in both 1 Thess. and Matt. 24 happen prior to the Wrath of God and those in Rev. 19 occur during it. We know with certainty that the rescue in 1 Thessalonians comes before the Wrath of God because we are told this directly (1 Thess. 5:9).

The events in the table are not just random events, but as we understand from Rev. 6, they are the first six seals of Revelation. This means the events in Matt. 24:4-30 are also the first six seals! Although these events are the same, there are other events that are missing in Matt. 24 that are found in Revelation. The Trumpet and Bowl Judgments found in Rev. 8, 9, 11, and 16 are the Wrath of God, and *not one* of these Judgements is found in Matt. 24. Yet Rev. 19:11-16 occurs *after* the Trumpet and Bowl Judgments. In fact, Armageddon is part of the final bowl! This is a striking difference between Matt. 24 and Rev. 19. Again, as with all the other comparisons, this precludes Rev. 19 from being the same event as Matt. 24. (or 1 Thess. 4-5).

## JESUS'S ROBES

There is one more proof we need to examine. It is a most unusual proof that verifies Jesus had been to the earth to pour out his Wrath *prior* to Rev. 19:11-16. If we read one of the beginning verses of this passage, we notice Jesus's robes are already stained before he leaves heaven:

> He is clothed with a robe dipped in blood, and His name is
> called The Word of God. (Rev. 19:13 NASB)

How did Jesus's robes become stained with blood? This is a reference to Isaiah.

> Who is this who comes from Edom, with garments of glowing
> colors from Bozrah, this One who is majestic in His apparel,
> marching in the greatness of His strength? "It is I who speak
> in righteousness, mighty to save." *Why is Your apparel red,*
> *and Your garments like the one who treads in the wine press?*

"I have trodden the wine trough alone, and from the peoples there was no man with Me. I also trod them in My anger and trampled them in My wrath; And their lifeblood is sprinkled on My garments, and I stained all My raiment. For the day of vengeance was in My heart, and *My year* of redemption has come." (Isa. 63:1-4 NASB, emphasis mine)

This is an astonishing passage in Isaiah. Nearly all Christians associate it with Jesus's return to fight Armageddon. But as we have just seen in Rev. 19:13, that is impossible because Jesus stained his robes *prior* to leaving to fight Armageddon. This passage in Isaiah has, by necessity, preceded Rev. 19:11-16. If Jesus was on or above the earth pouring out his Wrath prior to mounting his white horse in Rev. 19, when did this happen? The only plausible answer is after the prewrath rapture event in Matt. 24:29-31!

### WHICH ONES ARE ALIKE AND WHICH ONE IS DIFFERENT?
We have been playing the biblically correct version of "One of these is not like the others." I'm sure you will agree with me that the evidence is overwhelming! Not only are there significant similarities between 1 Thessalonians and Matthew, but there are also significant irreconcilable differences between Matt. 24 and Rev. 19.

There is only one possible conclusion. Matt. 24:29-31 is not the same event as Rev. 19:11-16, but is the same event as 1 Thess. 4:13-17. In fact, expressed in statistical terms, the odds of Matt. 24 and 1 Thess. 4-5 not being the same event approaches 1 in $\infty$ (infinity)!

Because Matt. 24:29-31 is, therefore, the Rapture and said to happen after the Great Tribulation, the pretribulation rapture is impossible.

PRETRIBULATION RAPTURE RESPONSE

Frankly, what can the pretribulation rapture theorists say in response? If the complete nature of this chapter was well understood, the rapture debate would be over. However, because the vast majority of the church has simply assumed that Rev. 19:11-16 and Matt. 24:29-31 are the same event, no significant research has been accomplished in this area. That is a pity. Hopefully, this book will shed light on this area because it effectively ends the Rapture timing discussion in favor of the prewrath rapture. However, in fairness, we will present what little evidence the pretrib. rapture camp has produced.

In an attempt to show that the passages in 1 Thess. 4-5 and Matt. 24 have irreconcilable differences, Dr. H. Wayne House wrote the following:

> The gathering in 1 Thessalonians is gathered together with Christ (and 2 Thess. 2:1 by previous reference of 1 Thessalonians 4) whereas the mention in Matthew 24 speaks only of being gathered together by angels, without reference to where the gathering occurs.[7] — Dr. H. Wayne House

Dr. H. Wayne House is the Distinguished Research Professor of Biblical & Theological Studies at Faith Evangelical Seminary in Tacoma, Washington,

---

[7] "Differences Between 1 Thessalonians 4 and Matthew 24," Pre-trib. Research Center, last modified unknown, accessed Jan. 2, 2018, http://www.pre-trib.org/articles/view/differences-between-1-thessalonians-4-and-matthew-24

President of Christian Perspectives International, as well as the author of numerous books and articles. And in his quote, he presents two ideas that he believes represent differences between the two passages (1 Thess. 4 and Matt. 24). These differences are:

- Believers are gathered by and to Jesus in 1 Thess. 4
- Angels do the gathering to an unknown destination in Matt. 24

First, before we address Dr. House's statement directly, I would like to point out that Dr. House makes mention of another passage, 2 Thess. 2:1, and asserts that the phrase "our gathering together to him" in this passage is a reference to the "catching up" (*harpazo*) in 1 Thess. 4:17. I agree. What Dr. House misses, however, is that the term "gathering together" in 2 Thess. 2:1 is the noun form of the Greek verb "gather together" (*episunago*) used in Matt. 24:31. So Matt. 24:31 is even a **stronger reference** to 2 Thess. 2:1 by using a form of this same Greek verb! Both are a "gathering together."

In direct response to Dr. House's statement, we need to examine a parallel passage to Matt. 24. As we mentioned in chapter two and as Dr. House acknowledges, Mark 13 is a second witness account of the events in Matt. 24. Although the passages in Matt. 24 and Mark 13 are nearly word-for-word, there are several differences which give nuanced understanding of the events.

> And then He (Jesus) will send forth the angels, and (Jesus) will gather together His elect from (*ek*) the four winds, from (*apo*) the farthest end of the earth to (*heus*) the farthest end of heaven. (Mark 13:27 NASB, clarification and emphasis mine)

First, notice that in this version of the events, it is clear that Jesus is doing the gathering (he is the subject of both verbs in the sentence.) Jesus uses the angels as the agents of his gathering, but he is doing it. This identical meaning should also be applied to Matt. 24:31. So in this way, Matt. 24:31 and 1 Thess. 4:16-17 are not different at all. Jesus does the gathering or snatching up of believers at the Rapture. The account in Matthew simply adds the additional piece of information that he uses his angels as agents to do the gathering.

Second, the direction of the gathering is given as from the earth to the "farthest end of heaven." Although, the English translation leaves some questions whether or not this is a directional statement, the use of three different prepositions in the Greek leaves no doubt. A more precise translation of these Greek prepositions would be: "will gather together his elect 'from out of' (*ek*) the four winds, 'away from' (*apo*) the farthest end of the earth 'up unto' (*heus*) the farthest end of heaven." Using this more precise translation, the directional aspect of the phrase becomes apparent.

If we assume the term "farthest end of heaven" means the atmospheric sky, then the gathering truly is to Jesus who is in the clouds. In this way, all aspects of Dr. House's critique are dispelled by this one verse, Mark 13:27.

However, can we go even further? Can we say the phrase "the farthest end of heaven" means the heavenly abode of God? This would be a de facto proof of the prewrath rapture in one verse because a gathering together to heaven, by definition, is the Rapture!

In order to establish this, we need to understand the Hebraic understanding of the term "heaven." They considered three "heavens." The first heaven was the sky, the second heaven consisted of outer space: the planets and stars, and the third heaven was the abode of God and his angels. Thus, the term, "farthest end of heaven," might be considered the highest heaven or this third heaven.

In Paul's second epistle to the Corinthians, he used an amazingly similar linguistic construction to discuss his own *harpazo* or "catching up" to the abode of God:

> I know a man in Christ who fourteen years ago—whether in the body I do not know, or out of the body I do not know, God knows—such a man was caught up (*harpazo*) to (*heus*) the third heaven. (2 Cor. 12:2 NASB)

First, there is an *harpazo* or gathering together. Second, the *harpazo* is up unto (*heus*) the third heaven. This phrase is almost identical to the order of words in Mark 13:27. Was this phrase in Mark the inspiration for Paul's wording in 2 Cor. 12?

Whether or not Mark 13:27 truly is a direct reference to a gathering together to the abode of God or not, I will leave to the reader to consider. It is a very interesting passage of Scripture, regardless. And it also completely dispels Dr. House's contentions about any dissimilarities between 1 Thess. 4-5 and Matt. 24.

## CONCLUSION

What almost no one has considered is that Scripture is quite clear that the "Second Coming" events in Rev. 19:11-16 and Matt. 24:29-31 cannot be the same occurrence. And if they are different events, Matt. 24 must be depicting the Rapture. It can't be anything else. This is re-enforced by the eleven direct similarities between it Matt. 24: 29–31 and 1 Thess. 4-5, as was shown in Figure 8. As we stated earlier, the odds that Matt. 24:29-31 isn't the Rapture approaches zero. Indeed, Matt. 24:31 is the greatest Scriptural misidentification of all time! It is describing the Rapture, and it happens after the Great Tribulation; therefore, definitively, the Rapture is not "pre-tribulational."

If you have been a follower of the pretribulation rapture, this is the moment your mind is instinctively looking for another "rabbit hole." It's human nature. And the most satisfying "rabbit hole" for the pretribulational position is the theory of imminence. How could anyone possibly disprove imminence?

That will be our task in the next chapter.

## Chapter Six

# CAN THE RAPTURE OCCUR AT ANY TIME?

## (Imminence)

*"But of that day and hour no one knows, not even the angels of heaven, nor the Son, but the Father alone."*

(Matt. 24:36 NASB)

The lynchpin doctrine of the pretribulation rapture position is the "imminent" return of Jesus to rapture the saints. The late Dr. Gerald Stanton outlines a definition of this theory:

The certainty that He may come at any moment, the uncertainty of the time of that arrival, and the fact that no prophesied event stands between the believer and that hour.[8]
— Dr. Gerald B. Stanton

Dr. Stanton was a pastor, author, founder of Palm Beach Atlantic University, professor for Moody Bible Institute, and the founder of Ambassador's International. And like most theories, his view of imminence has a grain of truth to it. As we discussed in the previous chapter, the precise day of Jesus's return is unknown. The quote of Matt. 24:36 above is the basis for this thought. It states that no man will know the day or the hour of his return. So the prewrath and pretrib. rapture position both concur on this one point.

---

[8] Gerald B. Stanton, *Kept from the Hour: Biblical Evidence for the Pretribulational Return of Christ*, 4th. Edition (Miami Springs, FL: Schoettle Publishing Co., [1956], 1991), p. 108.

However, these positions disagree on the concept that Jesus could come at any time and that no prophesied events stand between us and that return. When challenged to produce a passage from Scripture that clearly states this opinion, the pretribulationalists are not able to. "It is inferred," they say. By "inference," they mean that imminence is assumed based on logical (or illogical) suppositions made about Bible passages. Yes, that is all the pretribulationalists have to support their theory — suppositions.

This makes the theory of imminence a "phantom or ghost" theory. In fact, the pretribulation rapture itself is a phantom theory as well. There are no verses in the Bible clearly stating that Jesus will return before a seven-year Tribulation. Imminence is one phantom theory supporting another phantom theory (the pretribulation rapture).

## CHASING GHOSTS

One certainly can't prove a phantom or ghost exists, but it is just as hard to prove one *doesn't* exist. Just try proving a mythical creature like a ghost is a figment of one's imagination. It is harder than you'd imagine.

Scientists have utilized numerous methods to provide rational explanations of ghost sightings: measuring infrasound vibrations which can produce vague images, the ideomotor effect (unconscious muscle movement) leading to the Ouija board phenomenon, ions caused by radon gas, and hallucinations caused by carbon monoxide poisoning. But no matter how many ghost sightings are debunked, another ten will take their place.

This same principle has made the theory of imminence a resilient theory to disprove, which in turn has made it the most beloved "proof" of the pretribulation rapture theory.

One method that scholars have utilized to disprove it is to chase down every "ghost sighting," every inference of imminence proposed in scripture and prove it false. This is effective, but it certainly doesn't match our theme of simplicity! Additionally, for every ghost debunked, another is sighted!

Another method is to find a prophecy that must be fulfilled prior the Rapture of the church. This is where the phantom aspects of both imminence and the pretribulation rapture provide them protection. If there isn't a passage in scripture that identifies these phantom theories, there also isn't a passage that links them with signs or prophecies. Imagine the difficulty of finding a prophecy that must be fulfilled prior to a non-existent pretribulation rapture! Chasing imminence is very much akin to catching an invisible target.

Complicating this process even further is the idiosyncratic beliefs of many pretribulationalists that certain New Testament passages are "only for the Jews and not for Christians." Thus when a prophecy's fulfillment is during the Tribulation period (there are many), pretribulationalists will say that the Rapture has previously occurred and that the prophecy is only for the Jews.

However, God's Word is an endless resource, and in his infinite wisdom, he has provided an example that allows us to definitively disprove imminence with simplicity. Let's examine this most unlikely proof.

## IMMINENCE AND THE GREAT COMMISSION

Most Christians don't think of the Great Commission as a prophetic event, but it is.

> Go therefore and make disciples of all the nations, baptizing them in the name of the Father and the Son and the Holy Spirit, teaching them to observe all that I commanded you; and lo, I am with you always, *even to the end of the age.*"
> (Matt. 24:19-20 NASB, emphasis mine)

63

Jesus's promise at the end of this passage is both an assurance and a prophecy. It is a prophetic promise that Jesus will be with Christians until the end of the age. There is no question that Jesus directed this commission to all Christians throughout the ages. This is a thoroughly *Christian* (not Jewish) promise. By definition then, this is a prophecy that has not been fulfilled and won't be until the end of the age is realized.

But when is the "end of the age?" If we determine that it occurs during the Tribulation period, we will have our proof. The phrase is repeated five times in the book of Matthew. The most telling of all these references is found at the beginning of Matt. 24.

> As He was sitting on the Mount of Olives, the disciples came to Him privately, saying, "Tell us, when will these things happen, and what will be the sign of Your coming, and of *the end of the age*?" (Matt. 24:3 NASB, emphasis mine)

In response to this direct question from his disciples asking for a "sign" before the end of the age, Jesus responded with two references to this time that are considered signs:

> You will be hearing of wars and rumors of wars. See that you are not frightened, for those things must take place, but that is *not yet the end*. (Matt. 24:7 NASB, emphasis mine)

> This gospel of the kingdom shall be preached in the whole world as a testimony to all the nations, *and then the end will come*. (Matt. 24:8 NASB, emphasis mine)

So, Jesus is clear. There will be two signs that clearly occur before the "end of the age." The first, wars and rumors of wars (Revelation's second seal), is clearly stated to happen before the end. The second, the preaching of the gospel of the kingdom to all nations, is the sign after which "the end will come." So Jesus gave us two specific events. Both considered to be within the Tribulation (in Matt. 24) and that must occur prior to the end of the age.

**And this is the key point**: Jesus said he will be with us, the church, until that time. This is a double proof. One, it clearly shows Christians will be present in the Tribulation. And two, it discounts the main tenant of imminence, that no prophesied event must take place prior to the Rapture. Obviously, if the church is present, the Rapture has not yet taken place at the time of these events.

Additional references to the timing of end of the age are found in the parable of the wheat and the tares.

> The harvest is the *end of the age*, and the reapers are angels. Just as the weeds are gathered and burned with fire, so will it be at the *end of the age*. (Matt. 13:39-40 NASB, emphasis mine)

Jesus is clear that at the end of the age, the unrepentant will be burned with fire. This is certainly not a pretribulational event, nor even an event that occurs during the beginning of the Tribulation. It is an event that occurs on the Day of the Lord with fire falling at the first trumpet judgment. Jesus promises to be with his church up until that time. Therefore, his church is present on earth until that time as well!

Now, I'd also like to bring to your attention that in this verse, Jesus clearly states that the reapers of his Rapture harvest will be angels. In the previous chapter, Dr. House rejected this idea, and this verse in Matt. 13 is just one more piece of evidence that Dr. House was mistaken.

## MEANING OF MATT. 24:36

As has been the pattern, it is at this point that most will look for another "rabbit hole" proof. A most comforting rabbit hole is Matt. 24:36 which appears at the beginning of this chapter, and which may be the most misunderstood verse in the Bible.

> But of *that day* and hour no one knows, not even the angels of
> heaven, nor the Son, but the Father alone.
> (Matt. 24:36 NASB, emphasis mine)

This verse definitely states that the timing of Jesus's return is unknown. Pretribulation and prewrath theorists alike agree. But, that is not the same as saying no prophecies need to be fulfilled or that the Rapture can occur at any time.

Prior to the articulation of the prewrath rapture theory by Van Kampen and Rosenthal in 1990's, pretribulationalists used to use this verse to disprove the post-tribulation rapture theory. The end of the Tribulation period is believed by most to occur a set number of days (1260) after a specific event (the Abomination of Desolation). After that horrible, blasphemous event, the end of the Tribulation will be *a known day* and thus cannot qualify for the Rapture which must be *an unknown day*.

But prewrath scholars believe those days, the 1260 days, will be "cut short" or amputated (Gk. *koloboo*) for the sake of Christians (and only Christians). Jesus will rescue them prior to pouring out his wrath so they won't be present for the entire 1260 days.

Unless those days had been *cut short*, no life would have been
saved; but for the sake of the elect those days will be cut
short. (Matt. 24:22 NASB, emphasis mine)

How long before the end of the 1260 days will Jesus return to rescue his elect
Christians? It is unknown. This is the meaning of Matt. 24:36. No one knows
that day or hour.

Now although Matt. 24:36 is completely consistent with the prewrath
rapture, it is impossible, yes, I said it's *impossible* for it to refer to a
pretribulation rapture. This is a shock to almost everyone, I'm sure.

You see, most Christians mistranslate this verse as saying "no one
knows the day or the hour." There is even a famous, roadside billboard that
quoted this exact mistranslation!

## Figure 10: Mistranslated Billboard

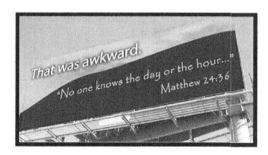

Now, turn back to look at the actual Bible verse. It states "of *that day* and hour
no one knows." There is an enormous difference between the actual verse and
the mistranslated billboard. The actual verse states we cannot know the timing
of *that day*. "That day" is a specific reference. Linguistically, it must refer
back to the last day that Jesus mentioned. It cannot refer back to a
pretribulation rapture that isn't mentioned (anywhere in Scripture). Matt.

24:36 cannot *under any circumstance* refer to a pretribulation rapture. It must refer back to Matt. 24:30-31, the last day that Jesus mentioned:

> Then the sign of the Son of Man will appear in the sky, and then all the tribes of the earth will mourn, and they will see the Son of Man coming on the clouds of the sky with power and great glory. And He will send forth His angels with a great trumpet and they will gather together His elect from the four winds, from one end of the sky to the other. (Matt. 24:30-31 NASB)

**By using "that day" in Matt. 24:36, Jesus clearly referred to the last day he mentioned: the prewrath rapture of Matt. 24:31 and not to a pretrib. rapture he never mentioned.**

By extension then, all other verses that follow "that day" and speak of an unknown day in Matt. 24 and the parallel accounts in Mark 13 and Luke 21 are referring to the prewrath rapture. In each instance, they are *not* referring to a pretribulation rapture that Jesus never mentioned. These other verses include:

> Therefore, be on the alert, for you do not know which day your Lord is coming. (Matt. 24:42 NASB)

> The Son of Man is coming at an hour when you do not think he will. (Matt. 24:44 NASB)

Of special interest is this verse found in Luke's version of Jesus's end time treatise:

> Be on guard, so that your hearts will not be weighted down
> with dissipation and drunkenness and the worries of life, and
> *that day* will not come on you suddenly like a trap; for it will
> come upon all those who dwell on the face of all the earth.
> But keep on the alert at all times, praying that you may have
> strength *to escape all these things* that are about to take place,
> and to stand before the Son of Man. (Luke 21:34-36 NASB,
> emphasis mine)

Notice this passage also speaks of "that day" just as Matt. 24:36, and it also mentions "escaping" (as in the Rapture), yet these references are to the prewrath rapture that is depicted in Luke 21:27, the last day Jesus mentioned, and not a pretribulation rapture found nowhere in Scripture.

Because Matt. 24:36 and the other unknown-day verses in Matt. 24, Mark 13, and Luke 21 don't refer to a pretribulation rapture, the most astute of the pretribulation rapture teachers such as Dr. Thomas Ice, Director of the Pre-Trib. Research Center, no longer consider any of these verses as indicating imminence[9].

## AN AWKWARD SITUATION FOR PRETRIBULATIONALISTS

Matt. 24:36 creates another extremely awkward situation for pretribulationalists. As we learned in the previous chapter, they claim that

---

[9] "Imminence and the Rapture (Part One)," Pretrib. Research Center, last modified unknown, accessed January 3, 2018, http://www.pre-trib.org/data/pdf/Ice-(Part1)ImminenceandT.pdf

Matt. 24:30-31 is the physical Second Coming when Jesus returns to fight Armageddon. And as we just learned in the previous section, they have also universally criticized post-tribulationalists because the physical Second Coming cannot be unknown given that it occurs a set number of days (1260) after the Abomination of Desolation. Yet we have just shown how the very event they say can't be unknown (Matt. 24:31 if it truly was the physical Second Coming) *is* unknown by the proofs we've just given.

Of course, the explanation is that Matt. 24:30-31 is not the physical Second Coming as pretribulationalists believe, and it has nothing to do with the end of the Tribulation. As we learned in the previous chapter, it is the prewrath rapture, and that is why it will occur on an unknown day! This is yet another proof that Matt. 24:30-31 is the Rapture not the physical Second Coming.

## THE BLESSED HOPE AND IMMINENCE

We need to debunk one additional "rabbit hole" proof because it represents a "type" of proof often quoted by pretribulationalists. Once it is understood why this isn't a proof for imminence, many other proofs will be debunked simultaneously.

Titus 2:13 refers to the return of Jesus as our "blessed hope," and it is! But this title, *the blessed hope*, has been adopted by pretribulationalists as a moniker for their pretribulation rapture.

> Looking for the blessed hope and the appearing of the glory
> of our great God and Savior, Christ Jesus (Titus 2:13 NASB)

No less a pretribulation luminary than the late Dr. John Walvoord has also utilized this verse as a proof text for imminence:

> The exhortation to look for the glorious appearing of Christ to
> His own loses its significance if the Tribulation must
> intervene first. Believers in that case should look for signs."[10]

Dr. Walvoord was a theologian, writer, pastor, and the past-president of Dallas Theological Seminary. He is still considered possibly the most prominent voice of dispensationalism in the world. However, despite his lofty position and academic credentials, his statement is far from a proof text. Rather, it is nothing but inference, and a failed inference at that.

It utterly fails because the context of Titus 2:13 demonstrates that the "looking" mentioned is about denying ourselves.

> Instructing us to deny ungodliness and worldly desires and to
> live sensibly, righteously and godly in the present age,
> looking for the blessed hope and the appearing of the glory of
> our great God and Savior, Christ Jesus. (Titus 2:12-12 NASB)

In context, we see that Paul is exhorting his protégé Titus to not consider worldly desires, but instead to consider (look forward to) the eventual coming of Jesus instead and the much greater rewards that would accrue then. The passage is about delayed gratification in light of the coming of Jesus.

As an example, during a college senior's final exams, one might say, "I bet you're 'looking to' getting that first job." This is the same usage of "looking to" as in Titus 2:13; it is a **looking beyond** current tribulation (final exams) to the blessed payoff (in the senior's case, a job).

---

[10] John F. Walvoord, The Rapture Question: Revised and Enlarged Edition (Grand Rapids: Zondervan, 1979), p. 273.

This is expectancy, not imminence. And Dr. Walvoord's inference error in this verse is repeated in nearly all the other passages that pretribulationalists use as "proofs" of imminence. For instance, Dr. Thomas Ice refers to this other verse as substantiation of imminence[11]:

> So that you are not lacking in any gift, awaiting eagerly the revelation of our Lord Jesus Christ. (1 Cor. 1:7 NASB)

The concept implied by pretribulationalists here is that one can only eagerly await the return of Jesus if the Tribulation doesn't intervene. Again, this is nonsense. In 2016, an infection damaged my heart. It required surgery and a two and one-half month recovery period. If you had asked prior to my surgery if I was eagerly awaiting my return to work, I would have told you, "YES!" This is despite the fact that life threatening surgery lay between where I was and my eventual return to work. If anything, my impending surgery made me long for a return to work all the more.

## THE BLESSED HOPE AND THE PREWRATH RAPTURE

What none of the pretribulationalists consider, however, is that Titus 2:13 is a proof text *for* the prewrath rapture! In order to understand how, we first need to examine the verse carefully because it is mistranslated in my NASB. An extra "the" has been added to the verse and this completely changes its meaning:

---

[11] "Imminence and the Rapture (Part One)," Pretrib. Research Center, last modified unknown, accessed January 3, 2018, http://www.pre-trib.org/data/pdf/Ice-(Part1)ImminenceandT.pdf

> Looking for the blessed hope and ~~the~~ appearing of the glory
> of our great God and Savior, Christ Jesus. (Titus 2:13)

In Greek grammar, when two nouns (such as hope and appearing) are connected by "and" and only the first noun is preceded by the definitive article "the," the words are related; both describing different aspects of the same thing. They are not separate thoughts[12]. In other words, our blessed hope *is* the glorious appearing of Jesus.

To that many pretribulationalists will say, "So what?" To them, Jesus appears to the church at the silent, pretribulation rapture. However, let's examine another verse that uses this same Greek term for the Rapture that we mentioned in the previous chapter, *epiphaneia* or "appearing."

> Then that lawless one (the Antichrist) will be revealed whom
> the Lord will slay with the breath of his mouth and bring to an
> end by the appearance (*epiphaneia*) of his coming (*parousia*).
> (2 Thess. 2:8 NASB, clarification mine)

By allowing Scripture to interpret Scripture, we see that at "the" one and only appearing of Jesus, he will bring the Antichrist to nothing (or to an end). Obviously, this is something that takes place during the Tribulation period. We also see this is at the *parousia*, the same *parousia* that in the last chapter we determined was in both 1 Thess. 4:13-17 and Matt. 24:29-31. This appearing is not a pretribulational appearing, but "the" appearing in which Jesus is revealed to the whole world in all his Shekinah glory, completely consistent with the wording of Titus 2:13, the "glorious appearing."

---

[12] Mathewson, David and Emig, Elodie, Intermediate Greek Grammar, (Baker Academic, Grand Rapids, 2016), p. 83.

So in this way, our *blessed hope* is the appearing in Glory of Jesus to the whole world as seen in Rev. 6:16 and Matt. 24:30. It cannot be a pretribulational rapture. Obviously, the Rapture of the church is our blessed hope. If the church had been raptured previously, nothing else could be our hope. In this way, the pretribulation rapture is disproven again. I find it ironic that the very title chosen by pretribulationalists is actually a proof against their theory!

## CONCLUSION

It is impossible to prove that a phantom exists, and pretribulationalists cannot prove imminence. It is also difficult to prove a phantom doesn't exist. It is like chasing down ghost sightings.

With the phantom theory of imminence, we have attempted to do that. We have shown that the main premise of imminence, that no prophecies must take place prior to the Rapture, is patently false. We have also shown that some of pretribulationalism's most cherished proof verses, Matt. 24:36 and Titus 2:13, actually demonstrate a prewrath rapture.

This concludes our study on the three defining questions. And we have demonstrated in three separate ways that only the prewrath rapture aligns with Scripture. There will be no pretribulation rapture. Believers will enter the Tribulation period.

# PART THREE:

## CONCLUSIONS

# Chapter Seven

# WHAT IF THE PREWRATH RAPTURE THEORY IS CORRECT?

*"Do not be conformed to this world, but be transformed by the renewing of your mind, so that you may prove what the will of God is, that which is good and acceptable and perfect. (Rom. 12:2 NASB)*

Intellectual and spiritual honesty come into play at this point. I'm sure you still have questions about rapture timing. I have studied the Rapture for years and still have questions. But the answers to the three defining questions preclude a pretribulation rapture. We don't need to answer every single question to know that the church will face the Tribulation. So the following uncertainty hangs in the air:

What is going to happen, and what do I need to do individually if the prewrath rapture theory is correct?

In the first chapter, we presented Rom. 12:2 quoted above, and discussed how the renewing of our minds is actually the changing of our minds. We are to leave behind our old theories and accept the truth of God's Word.

In this chapter, let's look at the last half of that verse, "So that you may prove what the will of God is." If I were writing that verse in my humanness, I'd have said to "know" what the will of God is. But the Apostle Paul chose the word "prove" (Gk: *dokimazein*). This word implies testing, analyzing, and examining. God wants us to dig into his word *after* we have changed our minds about old theories that were conformed to the pattern of this current age (the pretribulation rapture). This is exciting and challenging all at the same time.

God has a will for the end of the age. It is *his* will. And Romans tells us that his will is "good and acceptable and perfect." I came "out of" the pretribulation rapture position a number of years ago. I struggled greatly with accepting that God's will for Christians to enter the Tribulation period was "good and acceptable and perfect." I struggled because I was conformed to the pattern of this world that told me my safety and comfort were more important than my testimony and the gospel of the Kingdom. They aren't.

God's will for us is written on every page of Scripture. We are ambassadors for the coming Kingdom of Israel where Jesus will reign.

> God was in Christ reconciling the world to Himself, not counting their trespasses against them, and he has committed to us the word of reconciliation. Therefore, *we are ambassadors for Christ*, as though God were making an appeal through us; we beg you on behalf of Christ, be reconciled to God. (2 Cor. 5:19-20 NASB, emphasis mine)

God is making his appeal through us to the nations because he doesn't wish for any to perish (2 Pet. 3:9). And that ladies and gentlemen is the will of God for our lives, his good and acceptable and perfect will. It is not that we will be comfortable and safe — it's that all who can be saved will be saved, and he has given us the privilege to join him in this task.

And he will provide opportunities for us to do just that during the Tribulation that **may never be equaled during times of lesser persecution**.

But before all these things, they will lay their hands on you and will persecute you, delivering you to the synagogues and prisons, bringing you before kings and governors for My name's sake. *It will lead to an opportunity for your testimony.* (Luke 21:12-13 NASB, emphasis mine)

This passage from Luke's version of Jesus's end time treatise really strikes at the core of God's Will for the Tribulation. Although testimony of the saints isn't God's only purpose in the Tribulation, it certainly seems to be one of his primary ones. The word "testimony" is found in each of the Gospel versions of Jesus's end time prophecies and nine times in the Book of Revelation.

Let's examine several passages in Revelation where testimony is found:

I am a fellow servant of yours and your brethren who hold the *testimony of Jesus*; worship God. For *the testimony of Jesus is the spirit of prophecy.* (Rev. 19:10 NASB, emphasis mine)

This often-misunderstood passage lets us know that the work and worship of the servants of God is, in large part, this testimony about Jesus. Additionally, we learn all prophecy attests to Jesus and facilitates the testimony of the saints! These prophetic events (the Tribulation) will give Christians an opportunity for testimony just as Luke's Gospel foretells. The impact of this testimony is found in Revelation as well.

And they overcame him (the Dragon who is Satan) because of the *blood of the Lamb* and because of the *word of their testimony*, and *they did not love their life even when faced with death.* (Rev. 12:11 NASB, clarification and emphasis mine)

This is another often-misunderstood passage. Americans tend to be "rugged individualists" and look at this passage individually; how each Christian overcomes Satan in his own life. And although the passage can hold that meaning, I am rather convinced that John was looking at the overcoming as a corporate struggle of already saved Christians against the grip Satan has on the unsaved world. I believe Rev. 12:11 is an evangelistic message.

Satan's man, the Antichrist, is pictured as a rider on a white horse (coming as a "savior") in Rev. 6:2. In that verse, the same Greek word *nikao* (overcome) found in Rev. 12:11 is used. The Antichrist is said to be "overcoming and to overcome." The Tribulation is a battle of "overcoming;" the Antichrist and Satan are battling against Jesus and the church for the souls of the world. Who will overcome?

The church will overcome Satan in the Tribulation if they utilize the weapons at their disposal. The blood of the Lamb is the gospel message, and Christians' ultimate weapon. It both empowers the church and is its only message. Only Jesus saves. But the gospel needs to be spoken. Faith comes by hearing. So the second weapon is the testimony of the saints. Satan is overcome when the church speaks to the unsaved world.

The final weapon is the unpopular one, that the church must not love their lives even when faced with death. Just as the gospel needs to be spoken, the Tribulation will also require it to be spoken in difficult places and at the potential cost of one's life. To only speak it in "safe" situations will not overcome Satan.

This week I was listening to a contemporary Christian artist sing a wonderful gospel song that quoted Rev. 12:11. "And they overcame him

80

because of the blood of the Lamb and the word of their testimony." Over and over this portion of the verse rose and increased in intensity. It was a truly beautiful song. But something was missing.

What was missing in the song is what is missing in most of the evangelical church. Why is Islam growing faster than Christianity? Because not enough churches are training their congregations to "not love their lives even when faced with death." Many of the new generation of missionaries are not excited about taking the gospel where sharing it is a capital crime. This will be even more true during the Tribulation when these laws will become world-wide.

And the pretribulation rapture theory is partially to blame for this "easy" Christianity. At its core, it is escapist in nature. "Jesus loves us too much to allow us to enter the Tribulation and actually have to stand up for our faith," this culture is saying. I say Jesus loves us too much to not grant us that privilege.

## A NIGHT IN THE KINGDOM

And what a privilege it is! In my first book, *Are We Ready for Jesus?* (Seraphina Press, Minneapolis, 2015), I recounted a thought I had of what your future might be like. I'd love to share a paraphrase of it with you here.

After the Tribulation, Jesus will establish his Kingdom and those who are his ambassadors now will rule and reign with him. One night in that Kingdom, I imagined that you and I and several others will be huddled by a fire, warming our hands and talking about the days we spent in the Tribulation.

Out of the woods a shadowy figure joins us and warms his hands. As we look up, we suddenly realize it is the King, it's the King of all Kings, Jesus himself! But before we can say a word, he throws his arms around you and hugs you. To the rest of us he says, "You don't know this brother/sister like I do. He/she would never tell you what happened in my Tribulation, but I'd like to."

Then speaking only to you he said, "On that day, they brought you before the Antichrist himself. And in his arrogance, that man of sin decided to broadcast this moment to the world. He would show them what happens to those who love me. As a hundred million cell phones watched, the Antichrist asked you to deny me. Time and time again you refused. With each refusal, he had his henchmen beat you."

"But because you knew my word, rather than preparing what you would say on your own, you trusted the Holy Spirit to give you the words. The thought came into your mind to trick the Antichrist to allow one moment of testimony. You told him, "Okay, Okay, let me speak.""

"They let you stand up, and in a crystal moment of perfect Spirit-influenced clarity, you presented the gospel, the eternal gospel. The power of the words you were given stunned the cameramen. No one could move; even the Antichrist was frozen for a minute."

"I would like to show the result of that moment." Jesus then lifted his hands, and a vision of a vast multitude came into focus. "Great is your reward, my good and faithful servant," he said. "All of these, whom I love so dearly, are here in the Kingdom with us today because of my blood, the word of *your* testimony that shared my blood with the world, and that you didn't love your life even when faced with death."

Jesus then went to each of the rest of us around the fire and recounted the events of our time in his Tribulation. Although the impact of our testimonies was not as vast as yours, Jesus's love and satisfaction with us was just as great. And to me this is what Titus 2:13 is all about.

> Instructing us to deny ungodliness and worldly desires and to
> live sensibly, righteously and godly in the present age,
> looking for the blessed hope and the appearing of the glory of
> our great God and Savior, Christ Jesus. (Titus 2:12-12 NASB)

We "look forward" by spending every ounce of our strength in anticipation of the blessed hope and appearing of Jesus; living for that "night in the Kingdom" when Jesus shows us the results of our faith in him. Jesus is giving us an opportunity to share with him in his victory over the world and the Devil. Who wouldn't want to be blessed in this way? "Blessed are those who have been persecuted for the sake of righteousness, for theirs is the kingdom of heaven" (Matt. 5:10 NASB).

## LIKENED TO THE GHOST OF CHRISTMAS FUTURE

Jesus's words in Scripture show us visions of what is to come. Both the glorious fate of the saints who overcome and also the inglorious fate of those who fall away. Just as we saw in the prophecies of those who will overcome, the following is a prophecy about those who fall away:

> At that time *many will fall away* and will betray one another
> and hate one another. Many false prophets will arise and will
> mislead many. Because lawlessness is increased, *most
> people's love will grow cold.* (Matt. 24:10-12 NASB,
> emphasis mine)

Jesus is clear that many of those calling themselves Christians and attending our churches will "fall away" in the Tribulation and will even betray their fellow churchgoers into the hands of the Antichrist. In fact, Jesus states that

83

the love that most have for him and for others will "grow cold." He says "*most.*"

Now, in Charles Dicken's immortal classic tale, *A Christmas Carol*, the Ghost of Christmas Future showed Scrooge a vision of things yet to come. Scrooge asked the Ghost of Christmas Future, "Are these the shadows of things that will be or the shadows of things that might be?" Matt. 24:10-12 is a prophecy, and God's Word cannot be broken. This *will* happen. The only question is whether churchgoers in *your* church, small group, or family are going to fall away. Those are things that *might* be that you can influence.

Perhaps you are thinking, "My small group, most of my church, and all of my family are saved. Jesus isn't talking about them." Perhaps you are also thinking, "What does this have to do with Rapture timing?"

It is my opinion that ascribing to a pretribulation rapture position makes it more likely that someone will fall way or not overcome in end times because of a lack of preparation. Preparation or being ready for Jesus is what is important, and almost by definition, pretribulationalists do not prepare for what they don't think is going to happen. Let's examine why I believe this is so.

In a recent rapture timing debate between Alan Kurschner, a prominent prewrath expert, and Dr. Thomas Ice, Mr. Kurschner mentioned that if the pretribulation rapture position is mistaken, it is a great threat to the church. Dr. Ice responded that if it is mistaken, Christians will still dutifully go to a martyr's death just as saints throughout the ages have done. Dr. Ice's position is similar to that of multitudes of other pretribulationalists who believe that the pretribulation rapture theory is of no risk to the church, even if it is wrong[13].

---

[13] "Rapture Debate between Alan Kurschner (Pre-Wrath) and Thomas Ice (Pre-Trib.)," Eschatos Ministries, last modified September 27, 2015, accessed April 6, 2016,

Before we begin to study this topic in any depth, let me state my opinion up front that I believe once a Christian is saved, they are always saved. I don't believe a "born-again" Christian can lose their salvation; especially not because of their belief in any rapture theory!

## Born-Again Christians cannot lose their salvation

So in a manner-of-speaking, Dr. Ice is correct in his statement paraphrased above. Those who are saved will not deny Jesus and fall away. Their salvation is secure. But, this does not mean that the pretribulation rapture theory is not a risk to those attending our churches.

### THE RISK OF PRETRIBULATIONALISM

Jesus seems to indicate that not everyone who *thinks* they're saved, is saved. He also seems to indicate that those within our churches exhibiting this false faith may include up to 50% of church attendance. The eternal destiny of millions within our churches is a big deal!

Additionally, as you have just seen, those who are truly saved will have a sacred role to play in overcoming Satan and the Antichrist. It is likely that those who are unprepared will not know how to rise to the occasion and fulfill Jesus's specific commands for that time. So much is at stake for both the saved and the unsaved within our churches. We will discuss all the commands of Jesus that are currently being ignored by pretribulational churches in the next chapter. In this chapter, however, let's examine the risk to the vast number of unsaved in our churches' pews.

---

http://www.alankurschner.com/2015/09/27/rapture-debate-between-alan-kurschner-prewrath-and-thomas-ice-pretrib/ TIME: 1:19:10-1:19:30

Are 50% of those within our churches truly unsaved? In Jesus's teaching, he indicates that many of those who follow him are masquerading as Christians. They are the "tares" (that look like wheat). They are the trees producing bad fruit. They are the Church of Laodicea; not cold (unbelievers), but not hot (saved) either. And our churches all full of these "false" Christians.

These "false Christians" are the greatest mission field imaginable! They are within our churches, hopefully hearing the Word of God, and rubbing elbows with Christians every Sunday. They are also the ones Jesus indicates will "fall away."

## WEAK, HUMAN-BASED BELIEF

What does falling away mean? Jesus's first use of this term is found in the parable of the sower (Matt. 13:18-23) that he told during the early portion of his ministry. In that parable, Jesus elaborated on types of belief in the world. Jesus explained that the condition of people's hearts could be compared to different types of soil: "hardened," "rocky," "weedy," or "good." Unbelievers have "hardened" hearts. The saved have hearts that are like "good" soil. But in-between these polar opposites are two types of hearts ("rocky" and "weedy") that think they are saved, but are not.

Jesus further explained that those exhibiting this type of "weak, human belief" initially receive his Word with joy, but later can fall away:

> This is the man who hears the word and immediately *receives it with joy*; yet he has no firm root in himself, *but is only temporary*, and *when affliction or persecution arises* because of the word, immediately he *falls away*. (Matt. 13: 20-21 NASB, emphasis mine)

Jesus instructs us that "weak human-based belief" is only temporary, a surface type of belief. It is human-based and doesn't come from above because divine salvation is a permanent change — we are made new creations.

Those with "rocky" hearts may believe Jesus is the Son of God and even that he died for the sins of the world, but they aren't saved. Belief alone is not faith. "The demons also believe, and shudder" (Jam. 2:19 NASB). Faith is *acting* on that belief.

I can say I believe a bridge will support the weight of my car, but I don't have faith in the bridge until I drive over it. If I avoid the bridge and choose to not cross the river, I never truly had faith in the bridge, did I?

> Without faith it is impossible to please Him (God), for he who comes to God must believe that He is *and* that He is a rewarder of those who seek Him. (Heb. 11:6 NASB, clarification and emphasis mine)

We must not only believe that God exists, but also that he can support the weight of his promises! We are not saved by our works (what we do), we are saved by Jesus alone. It is the free gift of God. However, we *demonstrate* that we are saved and have faith by what we do. We must trust Jesus and "drive over the bridge." Otherwise it was never truly *saving* faith.

In Hebrews chapter 11, a long list of the faithful are described by how they demonstrated their faith. Noah built an Ark, Abraham left his homeland on God's command not knowing where he was going, and Sarah conceived the son promised despite her years because she and Abraham trusted God.

In contrast, those with "rocky soil hearts" will deny their belief in Jesus when persecution begins — it was never truly saving faith. They may consider themselves Christians, but when they face persecution (such as

87

during the Tribulation), they will "fall away" or renounce their belief. Their love for themselves exceeds their love for Jesus. Jesus uses this exact same term, "fall away," in the passage in Matt. 24:10-12 to describe what will happen to those with weak, human-based belief when their faith is tested before his return.

### ARE 50% OF CHURCHGOERS UNSAVED?

Jesus was *very* concerned about the falling away. When he concluded his teaching on the events before his return (Matt. 24), he told three parables to instruct Christians on how to apply his teaching. **These three parables are his primary application on how to prepare for his return**. All three involve those who think they are Jesus's followers ("slaves of the master" or "virgins"). Yet in each of these parables, a very significant percentage of those who think they're Christians "fall away."

In *the parable of the head of the house, the thief, and the master* (Matt. 24:45-51), there are two slaves of the master (Jesus). One of the servants provides for the master's household. The other slave "eats and drinks with sinners." (In a prophetic sense, this implies he takes the Mark of the Beast which signifies he has fallen away.) Upon the master's return, the unfaithful slave is cut to pieces and cast into the place of hypocrites where there is weeping and gnashing of teeth. "Hypocrite" is a word that means someone who pretends to be someone they aren't, like pretending to be a Christian.

In *the parable of ten virgins* (Matt. 25: 1-13), all ten "virgins" are keeping themselves pure awaiting the return of the bridegroom (Jesus). Yet five do not have enough oil (Holy Spirit) and their torches (Gk. *lampas*) burn out. For this reason, half of those eagerly awaiting Jesus's return do not enter the wedding feast.

In *the parable of the talents* (Matt. 25: 14-30), three slaves of the master (Jesus) are given a treasure of immeasurable value (the gospel). Yet the slave who hides his treasure is later cast into outer darkness.

All three parables involve contrasts between Jesus's followers who *think* they have faith and those who truly have it. The extreme events of the end times will test church goers. The testing of our faith reveals its nature: weak belief or saving faith.

In Matt. 25:10, Jesus calls those with saving faith those who were *ready*! If a vast number of those attending our churches are at risk of "falling away," doesn't it make sense to make them ready prior to facing the end times by discipling them? Preparing for the Tribulation is therefore an evangelistic mission, discipling those with "weak belief." The Holy Spirit may move in these sessions and millions with weak, human-based belief may be saved!

> **Preparing churchgoers to face the Tribulation is an evangelistic effort!**

### PRETRIBULATION RAPTURE AND THE "FALLING AWAY"

As we have stated, believing in an eschatological theory doesn't save or not save anyone. Millions of Christians who trust in pretribulationalism are saved, and many of these have incredibly strong faith. However, it is my opinion that pretribulationalism predisposes those with weak, human-based belief to fall way. It does this by prejudicing how its followers interpret the events unfolding before them.

In these days before the Tribulation, the escapist mentality that Jesus would never allow his followers to experience severe tribulation leads many churchgoers to avoid challenging situations even if these situations bring glory to God. In order to preserve their jobs, prestige, or lives, might one with an escapist mentality be more willing to compromise? I believe they would.

And during the Tribulation, someone with an escapist mentality would be much, much more likely to take the Mark of the Beast or deny Jesus if it meant death if they didn't. There are even some prominent pastors who teach that it is "okay" to take the Mark of the Beast[14].

So an escapist mentality as fostered by the pretribulation rapture theory predisposes a person to fail to live out their faith, both now and in the Tribulation.

Pretribulationalism will also cause those who have faith in it to misinterpret events in the Tribulation when they face them. If person has been told their entire life that they will not face the Antichrist or be asked to take the Mark of the Beast (an unforgivable sin), what will happen when they actually encounter these things? They will think, "This can't be the Antichrist or the Mark of the Beast as I've been taught Christians won't face these things. So even though this seems like the Mark of the Beast, it can't be." How much more likely will it be for them to commit apostasy?

Let's also examine what happens when a person who was discipled under a pretribulational doctrine *does* recognize the Antichrist. Will they ask, "If our church leaders were wrong about a doctrine so basic as whether or not

---

[14] "John MacArthur OUTRAGE: Take the Mark of Beast, still be saved. False Teaching." YouTube, last modified October 14, 2014, accessed January 6, 2018, https://www.youtube.com/watch?v=iU3tjRq6tX4
NOTE: Pastor MacArthur's ministry has issued a clarification on this subject, but did not recant his position, reiterating that taking the Mark of the Beast is not an unpardonable sin (see https://www.gty.org/library/Print/Blog/B131030). It is the position of this author that it is the Blasphemy of the Holy Spirit to take the Mark based on Scripture in Rev. 14 and Luke 12. For more information see http://www.thegospelintheendtimes.com/mark-of-the-beast/is-there-forgiveness-after-taking-the-mark-of-the-beast/

we would face the Tribulation, can I trust them about the divinity of Jesus?" When these disillusioned churchgoers then see the False Prophet performing demonically inspired miracles, will they commit apostasy?

Jesus has indicated that the "sign" Christians should look for is the Abomination of Desolation when the man of sin (Antichrist) sits in the Temple of God as if he is god. But those who ascribe to a pretribulational point of view do not study the signs and events that lead up to the Abomination of Desolation because they don't think they will see them. Thus, this event will take most of them by surprise. And because immediately after this horrible sign, the Great Tribulation will begin, most pretribulationalists will have the Great Tribulation take them by complete surprise as well without any time for emotional or spiritual preparation.

If one has spent their entire life anticipating a day when it is possible they will be asked to deny Christ, they likely will be ready for that day — to confess him before men whatever the consequences. They will have spent a lifetime of prayer and contemplation about that day and be ready. Those taken by surprise won't be ready. This was Jesus's warning in the parable of the ten virgins. The five foolish virgins were taken by surprise and their torches burned out. Only those who were ready went into the wedding feast.

## CURRENT CHURCH EFFORTS

Given the enormous risk of entering the Tribulation, one would think that many churches and organizations would be instructing their flock how to overcome Antichrist as a matter of safety, regardless of whether they believe they will face that time. However, this does not seem to be the case. A brief internet search demonstrates that most denominations and parachurch organizations have absolutely no online teachings about this subject. In fact, many present teachings that we can "take comfort" that we will not face Antichrist!

"So are these the shadows of things that will be or things that might be," Scrooge asked the Ghost? It is within our power right now to begin discipling our churches. We have time to make many "ready."

If you happen to be a pastor, elder, small group leader, Sunday School teacher, etc., I'd like to leave you with Jesus's warning to the heads of his household (the church). It is called the *parable of the head of the house, the thief, and the master* and is found in Matt. 24:43-51.

### JESUS WARNS CHRISTIAN LEADERS

First, it is important to also point out that this parable is not about a pretribulation rapture. As we mentioned in the previous chapter, after the return of Jesus on the clouds (Matt. 24:31), all the applications from that point on are referring to *that day* which is reference to the day Jesus comes on the clouds, not a pretribulation rapture that Jesus never mentioned.

Second, notice the parable is addressed to leaders of Jesus's household. In Matt. 24:45, we are told that the Master (Jesus) appointed a head of his household.

Third, notice that Jesus is instructing us that because we don't know the timing of his coming, our leaders must be ready at all times and also ready their churches.

> But be sure of this, that if the head of the house had known at what time of the night the thief was coming, he would have been on the alert and would not have allowed his house to be broken into. *For this reason, you also must be ready*. (Matt. 24:43-44 NASB, emphasis mine)

92

Jesus then demonstrates how to apply this teaching and be "ready." And he tells a riddle (Yes, Jesus told us a riddle):

> Who then is the faithful and sensible slave whom his master put in charge of his household to give them their food at the proper time? (Matt. 24:45 NASB)

Jesus asks "who" this is. "Who is the faithful slave?" Here are the clues:

- He is a slave, and a faithful one
- He is put in charge of his master's household
- He provides food for that household at the "appointed time"

Can you guess what Bible character fits these parameters? It's JOSEPH! Potiphar put the slave, Joseph, in charge of his house, and later Joseph fed all of Egypt with the grain that he stored away for the famine to come. Therefore, Christian leaders are to be "ready" for the 70th Week of Daniel by being like Joseph. If you haven't read any of my books, I'm sure this is a shock to you.

We will discuss how a Christian leader can be like Joseph for his flock in the next chapter, but for our purposes here, let's simplify the idea and say that he provides for his flock.

Jesus contrasts the faithful leader with an unfaithful one. In fact, Jesus refers to him as "evil." Here are the 3 reasons he is evil:

> But if that evil slave says in his heart, 'My master is not coming for a long time,' and begins to beat his fellow slaves and eat and drink with drunkards. (Matt. 24:48-49 NASB)

First, he doubts that Jesus is "right at the door" and coming soon. This is similar to Peter's comments about what "mockers" will say in the end times:

> In the last days mockers will come with their mocking, following after their own lusts, and saying, "Where is the promise of His coming?" (2 Pet. 3:3-4 NASB)

Why is it a sin to think Jesus is not coming soon? Obviously in Peter's day, Jesus wasn't coming soon! It has been two thousand years. And in Matt. 24: 36, 42, and 44 Jesus had just warned us multiple times that we can't know when he is coming. Why the shift in focus?

First, after the rise of Antichrist ("when you see the Abomination of Desolation" [Matt. 24:15]), all Christians watching for Jesus's return will know his coming on the clouds is 3.5 years away or less. So at that point, anyone asking, "where is the promise of his coming?" has ignored Jesus's instructions to "watch" and "be alert," and has failed to identify the Antichrist.

Second, this statement ignores Jesus's command that "you also be ready" at all times!

Think about the Christian leaders you know. How will they fare on this point? If they have been taught their entire life that they will not face the Antichrist, they may just think he is "another" world leader. This is a huge risk of pretribulationalism—— not watching for the signs of Jesus's return and thus not being able to recognize the Antichrist when he truly comes. This is the exact risk we described in the last section of this chapter.

In addition to not realizing that the church is within the Great Tribulation, how will evil church leaders "beat" their fellow slaves (Christians)? In Matt. 24:10, Jesus told us that many will fall away and betray one another and hate one another. And this parable *is* about falling away. It is a Christian leader (head of the house) who has fallen away. Will Christian leaders even betray the faithful Christians in their care who don't deny Jesus? I think it is a very likely (and frightening) possibility.

We also see that this leader eats and drinks with drunkards. This parable has a lot to do with food. We have already seen that the faithful leader provides for his flock. But, how will sinners eat during the Tribulation? They will have taken the Mark of the Beast to be able to buy food, so if this Christian leader is eating with them, he most likely will have taken the Mark as well!

Jesus then returns, and his punishment is swift:

> The master of that slave will come on a day when he does not
> expect him and at an hour which he does not know, and will
> cut him in pieces and assign him a place with the hypocrites;
> in that place there will be weeping and gnashing of teeth.
> (Matt. 24:50-51 NASB)

Notice the evil church leader is put in the place of other hypocrites, those that act as if they are Christians, but are not. This place of hypocrites will experience the Wrath of God which follows Jesus coming on the clouds and the Rapture.

SUMMARY

If you have spent your life thinking that "it doesn't matter what rapture theory we ascribe to, someday we'll all be with Jesus anyway," perhaps this chapter has helped open your eyes to the risks of the pretribulation rapture theory. And if you are a leader, remember that Jesus will hold us to a much higher standard. Hopefully, the first seven chapters of this book have helped inspire you to consider where you are leading your flock. Are you leading them to Jesus's Kingdom . . . or astray?

In the final chapter, we will examine Jesus's specific instructions to the faithful to overcome the Tribulation.

# Chapter Eight

# PREPARING THE CHURCH FOR THE TRIBULATION

*Rejoicing that they had been considered worthy to suffer shame for his name. And every day, in the temple and from house to house, they kept right on teaching and preaching Jesus as the Christ. (Acts 5:41-42 NASB)*

In the last chapter, we examined why it is important to prepare the church to face the Tribulation. Those with weak, human-based belief as opposed to true saving faith need to be evangelized, and those with saving faith need to be discipled so they can testify and overcome Satan and the Antichrist. In this chapter, we will present how Scripture instructs us to do so.

Yet despite the overwhelming evidence of how to prepare for that time found throughout the New Testament, many pretribulationalists still make statements like this:

> "The Bible never says anything or tells us any information on how to prepare for the Tribulation of the Antichrist. Wouldn't you think that a loving God would have done that, if indeed, we were to face that time?" — Eric Barger[15], Radio Talk Show Host

---

[15] "When Will the Believing be Leaving?" *Olive Tree Ministries*, last modified November 25, 2017, accessed January 6, 2018, https://www.youtube.com/watch?v=4UCuD8AKmTk, TIME 0:0:25 – 0:0:41

There was a time when the knowledge of Scripture was so prevalent in the church that a statement like this would have gotten someone laughed off of the stage. But in today's world of "easy Christianity," pulpit messages downplay end times, and many churchgoers might accept a statement like this. That makes Barger's statement very, very dangerous. The reason being, of course, the risks of not preparing found in the previous chapter.

This entire chapter is a response to Mr. Barger's comment. However, his statement is so egregious, it requires an immediate, brief reply. The following are twelve (12) commands for the Tribulation period found soley in Matt. 24:

### Figure 11: Jesus's Commands in Matt. 24

| Jesus's Commands | Matt. 24 |
|---|---|
| See to it that no one misleads you. | 24:4 |
| See that you are not frightened | 24:6 |
| Give them their food at the proper time | 24:45 |
| Then those who are in Judea must flee to the mountains. | 24:15-16 |
| Whoever is on the housetop must not go down to get the things out that are in his house. Whoever is in the field must not turn back to get his cloak. | 24:17-18 |
| But pray that your flight will not be in the winter, or on a Sabbath. | 24:20 |
| Then if anyone says to you, 'Behold, here is the Christ,' or 'There he is,' do not believe him. | 24:23 |

| Jesus's Commands | Matt. 24 |
|---|---|
| So if they say to you, 'Behold, he is in the wilderness,' do not go out, or, 'Behold, he is in the inner rooms,' do not believe them. | 24:26 |
| Now learn the parable from the fig tree | 24:32 |
| When you see all these things, recognize that he is near, right at the door. | 24:33 |
| Therefore be on the alert, for you do not know which day your Lord is coming. | 24:42 |
| For this reason you also must be ready | 24:44 |

Now Mr. Barger may erroneously claim that Matt. 24 is "only for the Jews," but it is unmistakable that in it, Jesus has provided readers of his Word with numerous commands and specific information to assist them in overcoming the Tribulation. And Matt. 24 is only one chapter of one book of the Bible. As you will soon see, there are dozens of commands and suggestions for overcoming the Tribulation.

**TEAM PREPARATION**

College Basketball is a huge sport in my home state of North Carolina. Duke, North Carolina State, UNC, Wake Forest, and, of course, my hometown University of North Carolina at Wilmington (UNCW), dominate discussions between October and March Madness. Just as the coaches of these fine schools would never consider preparing each player individually without team preparation, in the same way, our churches require "team preparation" for the Tribulation.

The first century church described in the Book of Acts is a wonderful model church upon which to base our future Tribulation churches. Additionally, Jesus's letters to the seven churches found in Rev. Chapters 2-3 are directed to the church as it endures the Tribulation, giving advice about that time period. If you would like an explanation of why that is so, over one-hundred pages of my second book, *Revelation Deciphered* (Ready for Jesus Publications, Wilmington, 2016) are dedicated to this subject.

We will refer to both of these sections of Scripture throughout this chapter because corporate preparation is essential to overcoming.

### THE CHURCH OF ACTS

The church that first formed in Jerusalem after Peter's sermon on Pentecost has traditionally been thought of as a "pure" church unpolluted by the world. It has been considered an ideal model to base any Christian fellowship or ministry. If the church in the Tribulation is going to overcome, it will need to emulate the church of Acts in many ways.

There was a short period of time before the persecution of that first-century church began, and the features of that first church helped it overcome the later persecution. The church in America is still not undergoing severe persecution. If it were to adopt the features of the church in Acts 2 now, it would be better prepared for the persecution that will eventually come. Let's look at those features of the early church and find out why they were important to later success.

> They were continually devoting themselves to the apostles' teaching and to fellowship, to the breaking of bread and to prayer. . . they began selling their property and possessions and were sharing them with all, as anyone might have need.

Day by day continuing with one mind in the temple, and
breaking bread from house to house, they were taking their
meals together with gladness and sincerity of heart (Acts 2:42,
45-46 NASB)

There were four aspects to the initial development of the church:

- Daily teaching of the Word
- Fellowship and sharing of meals
- Prayer
- Communal finances

The early church "devoted" themselves to these things. Notice they were in
the temple daily and shared meals together. Just imagine the advantage such a
church would have in preparing its members to face persecution! In our
modern world, however, the self-absorbed culture of western countries would
probably cause this type of organization to fail. However, astute church
leaders may begin to organize their churches with this model in mind now,
realizing that God may radically change world-wide events in an instant,
necessitating such church organization. Churches that have begun the process
will be much more prepared for full "overnight" implementation.

Regardless of whether churches can accomplish such organization
immediately, this model is presented in this chapter because it will be the "go-
to" model in the Tribulation. As we work thru each portion of preparation, we
will continually refer back to this structure and how it will facilitate corporate,
not just individual preparation.

### THE ENEMY'S BATTLE PLANS

An enormous advantage that the church holds in preparing for the Tribulation is that we know the enemy's battle plans in advance! In the American Civil War, the Confederate forces' battle plans for the Antietam campaign were wrapped around three cigars. Inadvertently, they were left behind when the confederates broke camp. Union soldiers found the plans and turned them over to Union General George B. McClellan, but he was slow to act, and the advantage the intelligence provided was lost.

That is exactly how I feel about the advantage our Lord has given us to prepare for the Tribulation. Satan and the Antichrist's main strategic ideas are all mapped out for the church in the Gospels and Revelation. However, rather than utilizing the enemy's battle plans to prepare ourselves, our churches have become bogged down in the mire of constant bickering and arguing. In a desperate attempt to prove their theory right, some claim that these battle plans and our instructions to overcome them don't even exist!

This "battle plan" is outlined in the first five seals of Revelation. As we saw in Figure 9 of chapter five, the Gospel accounts of Matt. 24, Mark 13, and Luke 21 exactly parallel these seals. In addition to the Gospels, what is seldom recognized is that the Letters to the Seven Churches in Rev. 2-3 are prophetic and also parallel the seals. Each letter gives advice to the Church as they attempt to overcome each of the seals (the Church of Ephesus is about the first seal, etc.). In combination, these chapters of the Bible provide Christians with everything our Lord felt we needed to know in order to prepare.

This chapter will be organized in this same way. The first sections will deal with how the church needs to prepare for the first seal, the second sections will deal with how to prepare for the second seal, etc.

## DECEPTION AND THE CHURCH OF THE FIRST SEAL

After the first seal Jesus told us that false messiahs will arise:

> See to it that no one misleads you. For many will come in my name, saying, "I am the Christ," and will mislead many . . . For false Christs and false prophets will arise and will show great signs and wonders, so as to mislead, if possible, even the elect. Behold, I have told you in advance. So if they say to you, "Behold, *He* is in the wilderness," do not go out, *or*, "Behold, *He* is in the inner rooms," do not believe them. (Matt. 24:4–5, 24–26 NASB, emphasis mine)

Jesus has specifically informed us that his *parousia* will be like lightning from the east to the west (Matt. 24:27). It will be unmistakable, and it will follow the darkening of the sun and moon (sixth seal), which will also be unmistakable.

However, Jesus warns us that false messiahs and prophets will arise prior to these events. These false messiahs *may* claim to be Jesus himself (they will come in his name) and will perform great signs and wonders. This will be such a great deception that only those who are spiritually prepared will be able to resist. Jesus said the false messiahs will mislead many, and if possible, *even the elect*. These signs will not be magic tricks; they will be demonically empowered wonders. Those within the church that are attracted to signs and wonders and who are not discerning will be especially vulnerable.

The Muslims expect Jesus to return in the person of Isa (the Muslim Jesus). If he arises, this *false* Jesus will support the claims of the Mahdi, the Muslim Messiah. The Jews expect two messiahs: Messiah ben Joseph and

Messiah ben David. Should demonically empowered men arise to fill these roles prophesied by the heretical Muslim Scriptures and the teaching of the Jewish rabbis, the deception may be great indeed. We must prepare our churches for what the *true* signs will be.

As we mentioned above, Jesus's letter in Revelation to the ancient Church of Ephesus was both a letter to the historic church and a letter to modern Christians who will endure the first seal. If you have questions about this interpretation, the Scriptural rationale for it is outlined in my aforementioned book, *Revelation Deciphered*, chapter four.

In the Letter to Ephesus, Jesus commends the church for "testing" false prophets and proving them false.

> You put to the test those who call themselves apostles, and
> they are not, and you found them to be false. (Rev. 2:2
> NASB)

This will be one of the two important tasks of that future church at the beginning of the Tribulation. As we mentioned above, very convincing imposter prophets and Christs will arise. They will look good, they will sound like the real thing, and in terms of the Antichrist, he will bring peace to the Middle East. He will be loved and respected by the cultures of the world. He will be a rider on a white horse, overcoming and attempting to overcome (Gk. *nikao*).

Something *may* also happen to discredit the Gospel accounts to cast doubt on the real Jesus. It will be very easy for churchgoers to get swept up in the mania surrounding the Antichrist; very easy. The task of the Church of the First Seal will be to identify the false prophets as *false*.

Christians who are fellowshipping and studying daily in a Church of Acts setting will find it so much easier to accomplish the tasks before them after the first seal. The encouragement of many other spirit-filled believers will be of upmost importance. In addition to identifying false prophets, it's other primary task will be to intensify our love for our Lord.

> But I have this against you, that you have left your *first love*. Therefore remember from where you have fallen, and repent and do the deeds you did at first. (Rev. 2:4–5 NASB, emphasis mine)

## ALL WE NEED IS LOVE

We all must do a self-assessment of our relationship to our Lord. No one will overcome Satan or the Antichrist without a sold-out love for Jesus.

**All other preparation springs from our love for Jesus.**

The Greek word *agapao* (*agape*) means loving what we place first in our lives, what totally consumes us and drives us. This is the type of love God expects. Things that we *agapao* may include careers, family, money, comfort, houses, or self.

Do you love (*agapao*) God? Most of us would automatically say, "Yes, of course!" But, how often do we put his will and his desires above our own? Are we consumed and driven by what he desires for our life and not what we want? Is our own happiness more important than what *God desires* for our lives? We all must be brutally honest when we answer these questions. No one will be able to overcome the Tribulation without the infilling of the Holy Spirit and a sold-out devotion to Jesus.

How do we develop this type of love? First, all relationships arise from time spent with the person. Nothing will substitute for reading Scriptures, fasting and praying, and working alongside our Master serving his children. We must first have a relationship with Jesus.

But a relationship with our Lord is not the same as *agapao* love for God. *Agapao* love means a loss of self, a setting aside all our own thoughts, emotions, and desires that are contrary to God's will. *Agapao* means denying yourself and taking up your cross.

> He was saying to them all, "If anyone wishes to come after Me, he must deny himself, and take up his cross daily and follow Me. *For whoever wishes to save his life will lose it, but whoever loses his life for My sake, he is the one who will save it.*" (Luke 9:23–24 NASB, emphasis mine)

We are all familiar with the above passage; the one who tries to save his life will lose it. In church-world, we think of this in relation to serving our church families, giving our tithes, etc. We also think of this in terms of our lives within our own families, sacrificially loving our spouses and children. All of these things are wonderful. However, the days are coming when self-denial for the sake of Jesus will take on a different, more intense character.

In the times that are coming upon the world, there will be powerful pressure to deny Jesus; it is the essence of apostasy. The only defense against this enormous pressure to commit apostasy will be *agapao* love for our Lord. Jesus's restoration of Peter after his denial explains how this works.

## PETER'S *AGAPAO* LOVE (A CASE STUDY)

Most Christians know that Peter denied Jesus three times on the night he was betrayed. After Jesus's resurrection, he restored Peter in a passage where he asked him three times whether Peter loved him. Let's look at the specific passage:

> So when they had finished breakfast, *Jesus said to Simon Peter*, "Simon, son of John, do you love [Gk: *agapao*] me more than these?" He said to Him, "Yes, Lord; you know that I love [Gk: *philo*] you." He said to him, "Tend My lambs." He said to him again a second time, "Simon, son of John, do you love [Gk: *agapao*] me?" He said to Him, "Yes, Lord; you know that I love [Gk: *philo*] you." He said to him, "Shepherd My sheep." He said to him the third time, "Simon, son of John, do you love [Gk: *philo*] me?" Peter was grieved because He said to him the third time, "Do you love [Gk: *philo*] me?" And he said to Him, "Lord, You know all things; you know that I love [Gk: *philo*] you." Jesus said to him, "Tend My sheep." (John 21:15–17 NASB)

This is a very interesting portion of Scripture. Notice that John refers to Peter as Simon Peter, whereas Jesus only refers to him as Simon. In some ways, this contrast of names shows Jesus may have been trying to say that Peter had regressed to a level that he was at before Jesus gave him the name Peter ("Rock"). (This naming of Peter was the result of Peter's confession of Jesus as Messiah [Matt. 16:16–18].) Peter's later denial resulted in the removal of the name. Denial of Jesus is apostasy. Peter had a long road to climb to restoration.

Second, Jesus asked Simon Peter if he loved him more than "these." The phrasing is a bit ambiguous and could mean Peter's profession (fishing), or Jesus could be asking if Peter still thought he loved him (Jesus) more than the other disciples did. On the night he betrayed Jesus, Peter had bragged that even though all the others would reject Jesus, he would not (Matt. 26:33). I rather like this second meaning because it would mean that Jesus was reminding Peter of his past failing (as he restores him). He also showed it was a failure of *love*. After each of Jesus's questions, he asked Peter to demonstrate his love by "feeding" (spiritually nourishing) Jesus's followers (the lambs).

Also notice the Greek words translated "love" give this passage an incredibly different meaning in the Greek as opposed to the English. The words that Jesus used for the first two occurrences of "love" are more intense (*agapao*) than Peter's (*philo*). As we have seen, *agapao* can be thought of as godly love, while *philo* can be thought of as brotherly love. The first two times Jesus asked Peter if he loved him, Jesus used *agapao*, but Peter only replied that he loved Jesus with a brotherly love. Most likely, he was embarrassed by his failure and didn't want to claim the higher level of love Jesus was asking about. Finally, on the third question, Jesus lowered the standard of love he asked about. This third time he asked Peter if he loved him like a brother. Peter became angry at this lowering of the standard and told Jesus, "You know I love you like a brother." *Philo* love is given to those you know and like and who like you in return. But maybe Peter got angry because he remembered Matthew 5:46 where Jesus said, "If you love those who love you, what reward will you get? Are not even the tax collectors doing that?" Jesus then explained to Peter that he was going to need a higher standard of love if he was not going to fall away again.

"Truly, truly, I say to you, when you were younger, you used to gird yourself and walk wherever you wished; but when you grow old, you will stretch out your hands and someone else will gird you, and bring you where you do not wish to go." Now this He said, signifying by what kind of death he would glorify God. And when He had spoken this, He said to him, "Follow Me!" (John 21:18–19 NASB)

In this way, Jesus was telling Peter (and us) that *philo* love would not be enough. *Agapao* love was going to be necessary in the future in order for Peter (and us) to overcome and become victorious.

As we know, Peter became a leader of the church, a great evangelist, and a writer of two epistles that bear his name. He also overcame his trial at the end of his life. Tradition tells us that he was crucified upside down on a Roman cross. Jesus does not remove all from the trial; to some he says, "Follow me."

If Peter fell away after spending three and a half years with our Lord, we must beware to arrogantly say (as Peter did) that we would die first before betraying our Lord. Rather, we need to pray that we will all be filled with *agapao* love for Jesus to the point where we lay our own interests aside. The pressure to commit apostasy during the Tribulation will leverage everything: our jobs, homes, food, family, our very lives, etc. If we value anything higher than Jesus, we risk falling into apostasy. Most in the Western church today "love" Jesus. But do they love Jesus more than their spouses and children? Do they love Jesus more than their jobs; or is their love just *philo* love?

109

*Knowing* that we will face the great tribulation is a wonderful blessing! Thinking about that trial helps us focus on our relationship to Jesus and what it will take to overcome. This is why the pretribulation rapture theory is such a trap; it allows its exponents to believe they can enter the kingdom with less than a sold-out, *agapao* love for Jesus. It allows them to think they can get by without giving up everything to follow him. **Proper understanding of rapture timing, however, blesses us by allowing us to devalue the things of this world**, which we will only leave behind anyway.

> *Be Thou my Vision, O Lord of my heart*
> *Naught be all else to me, save that Thou art*
> *Thou my best Thought, by day or by night*
> *Waking or sleeping, Thy presence my light*[16]

## WAR, CHAOS, AND THE CHURCH OF THE SECOND SEAL

The second seal events are war and chaos, both of which lead to fear. Fear is an overriding emotion. God anticipates that people will be fearful from the second seal on. That is why he instructs us, "See that you are not frightened, for those *things must take place*" (Matt. 24:6 NASB, emphasis mine). Jesus is telling us that he has all things under his control; that these *things must take place* before the kingdom is ushered in.

Fear of pain and death are at the top of the list of our human fears. In the letter to Smyrna, the Church of the Second Seal, Jesus lays these fears wide open; he tells us we should *anticipate* prison and death:

---

[16] *Be Thou My Vision*, Verse One, traditional Irish hymn "Rop tú mo Baile," English text by Eleanor Hull

*Do not fear what you are about to suffer.* Behold, the devil is about to cast some of you into *prison*, so that you will be tested, and *you will have tribulation for ten days. Be faithful until death, and I will give you the crown of life* . . . He who *overcomes* will not be hurt by the *second death*. (Rev. 2:10–11 NASB, emphasis mine)

Jesus has let us know these are *things that must take place*. The Tribulation is not an accident; it is the sovereign will of Jesus. And Jesus has prepared a role for us in it, but in order to assume that role we must not fear:

But for *the cowardly* and unbelieving and abominable and murderers and immoral persons and sorcerers and idolaters and all liars, their part will be in the *lake that burns with fire and brimstone*, which is the *second death*. (Rev. 21:8, emphasis mine)

Notice that the first category of those who will face the second death are the cowardly. This is incredible! How many Christians in our Western churches are *expecting* to lay their lives down for Jesus and the gospel? How many will be *afraid* and *frozen* from proper action or hide when the time comes to choose life or faithfulness? Jesus expects us to follow his command and *love him more than our own life*. "For whoever wishes to save his life will lose it, but whoever loses his life for My sake, he is the one who will save it" (Luke 9:24 NASB). God expects us to bring his gospel to a dying world regardless of the cost. During the second seal, he specifically commands us to not be frightened:

111

You will be hearing of wars and rumors of wars. *See that you are not frightened*, for *those things* must take place, but that is not yet the end. For nation will rise against nation, and *kingdom against kingdom*. (Matt. 24:6–7 NASB, emphasis mine)

Jesus warns Christians to not be frightened because events that surround this sign would frighten most people. This fear will drive more unsuspecting people into apostasy, causing them to worship the Antichrist. This is why this warning is so important—we must never worship the Antichrist.

They worshiped the beast, saying, "Who is like the beast, and who is able to wage war with him?" (Rev. 13:4 NASB, emphasis mine)

Notice that it is the Antichrist's prowess in war that leads many to worship him.

## FAMINE AND THE CHURCH OF THE THIRD SEAL

*Riches I heed not, nor man's empty praise*
*Thou mine Inheritance, now and always*
*Thou and Thou only, first in my heart*
*High King of Heaven, my Treasure Thou art*[17]

The third seal will usher in famine and economic collapse. The church is divided on whether we should prepare for the apocalypse to come. Some are putting away gold, groceries, and guns and planning to be ***survivalists***. Others

---

[17] *Be Thou My Vision*, Verse Four, traditional Irish hymn "Rop tú mo Baile," English text by Eleanor Hull

plan to trust that God will supernaturally provide in days that are approaching and aren't preparing at all. So, what does Scripture say? Is there a verse in the New Testament in which Jesus clearly teaches that we should put food away for the hard times? Does Jesus want Christians to become preppers? Shockingly, the answer is yes, and there *is* a verse that supports this idea— Matthew 24:45 which we have already studied:

> Who then is the faithful and sensible slave whom his master put in charge of his household *to give them their food* at the proper time [Gk: *kairos*, meaning "appointed time")? (Matt. 24:45 NASB, emphasis mine)

As a church, we tend to read past this highly important yet obscure verse found in Matthew. As we mentioned in the previous chapter, Jesus was giving us a riddle. He is asking *"Who* is this wise and faithful slave?" We have three clues:

- He is a wise slave
- He is put in charge of his master's household
- He provides food for that household at the appointed time

As we saw in chapter seven, the answer is Joseph, the wise and faithful slave that Potiphar put in charge of his household (Gen. 39:1–6) and, later, that Pharaoh put in charge of Egypt (Gen. 41:33–57). Joseph provided food for that household, both Hebrews and Egyptians, as well as later, for all of Egypt in the seven-year famine. Once we solve the riddle of this verse, its meaning opens up to us: Jesus wants us to be Joseph for *his* household in the coming "appointed time."

We need to stop and pause. Jesus wants us to be a Joseph for his household? Yes, he does. He doesn't want us to only prepare for our own household, but for *his household*. There is an incredible difference. Christians who are preppers for their own households store up gold, guns, and groceries for themselves. Many plan to escape the hard times and hide in a mountain retreat or a bunker. I call these persons "*survivalists.*" Jesus is calling us to provide for his household: *both the Jewish remnant and the church.* I call the persons who will sacrificially provide for the "least of these" during hard times "*revivalists.*"

Jesus also indicates that he wants us to provide this food at a specific time, and it is critically important to understand what this time is. Joseph stored food and provided it during the "appointed time" of the seven-year famine that occurred in the Middle East in those days. In so doing, he saved the lives of his brothers and their families in addition to saving numerous Egyptians. Jesus is calling us to provide his household with food during the coming appointed time. What might that time be? Just a few verses earlier in Matt. 24, Jesus taught the disciples that there would be famines during the beginning of the birth pangs period (the first three and a half years of the Tribulation). Might this be the appointed time? I believe it is.

We also know that the False Prophet will institute the mark of the beast during the Seventieth Week:

> He causes all, the small and the great, and the rich and the poor,
> and the free-men and the slaves, to be given a mark on their right
> hand or on their forehead, and he provides that no one will be able
> to buy or to sell, except the one who has *the mark*, either the name
> of the beast or the number of his name. (Rev. 13:16–17 NASB,
> emphasis mine)

Is the mark of the beast directly tied to the famines? Do the False Prophet and Antichrist take advantage of the food shortage to offer a "solution" in the form of a new economic system that provides food? **We know that taking this mark and participating in this economic system leads to eternal damnation (Rev. 14:9-12). This is important stuff.**

If this scenario is accurate, millions or billions of hungry people might readily take the mark to avoid starvation. What if Christians had food stored up and were able to provide it to some of those in need at this time? Would this stored food be an impetus for the needy to reject the Mark of the Beast and come to faith in Jesus? It is an interesting and intriguing theory. In Jesus's letter to the church at Pergamum, the Church of the Third Seal, we read:

> But I have a few things against you, because you have there *some* who hold the teaching of Balaam, who kept teaching Balak to put a stumbling block before the sons of Israel, *to eat things sacrificed to idols* and to commit *acts of* immorality. (Rev. 2:14 NASB)

First, notice Jesus says there are "some" in the church who hold to false teaching, and Jesus holds this against the *entire* church. This clearly teaches Jesus holds us responsible for his entire household. Second, part of the false "teaching of Balaam" was to cause Israel to eat unholy food that was sacrificed to idols. In a modern analogy, might this be food purchased through the Mark of the Beast? Might prepared Christians be able to help their fellow brothers and sisters resist the mark if they have food to share?

This is the point at which a light bulb may be going off for you as it did for me. If our churches were organized like the Church of Acts, they would be communally sharing their financial provision. If they anticipated the coming famines as they should, they would have put food away for this coming time of testing using shared resources.

## PACK YOUR LUNCH

But, how will we ever be able to provide food for our entire church, you might ask? You won't be, obviously. But you might be able to "pack your lunch." Jesus's feeding of the five thousand is instructive. The disciples first came to Jesus and recommended he send the crowds away to find food. Jesus then asked the disciples to feed them. The puzzled disciples were only able to find a young boy with a lunch of two fish and five loaves. From this simple lunch, Jesus miraculously multiplied the food and was able to feed the huge crowd.

The faith of this boy who packed his lunch and willingly gave it to the Master to distribute to help feed the crowd was what Jesus desired to see. From this simple act, the crowd experienced a great miracle. If we "pack our lunch" and willingly give it to others during the appointed time, will Jesus multiply our efforts? I think this well may be the case.

This also brings up the point of solely relying on the provision of God *without effort on our own*. Jesus acted upon the faith of the young boy. The boy packed food because he knew he'd need it. He planned to stay and listen to Jesus as long as he could, and he planned in advance to do so by packing a lunch. He then willingly surrendered all he had. We know there will be famines; Jesus has told us as much. Isn't it presuming upon the Lord to believe he will provide for us without any effort on our parts to contribute to that provision? Yes, Jesus will provide for us, but don't we share in the responsibility to do what we can, and then to rely on him to do what only he can? We observe that pattern repeatedly in Scripture.

When the appointed time comes, there will be many more important issues than our survival. Once the Tribulation begins, the great countdown to the return of our King will also begin. We will be entering the two-minute warning, to use a football analogy. Strategies we have employed previously will need to be modified.

"*Revivalist*" preppers and prepper churches will step out in faith and use the food they have stored up to bolster the faith of those who haven't prepared. In this way, they likely will participate in a great miracle and possibly the salvation of many souls. The "food" they provide will likely be physical food as well as "spiritual" food in terms of the gospel!

"*Survivalist*" preppers will horde their food and attempt to survive at all costs. With Jesus's return only a few years away at that point, does that even make sense? Do you want to spend your last days hiding in a bunker eating beans, or do you want to participate in the great spiritual battle against Satan and the kingdoms of this world that will "prepare the way of the Lord?" Which prepper will you be?

## THE ABOMINATION AND THE CHURCH OF THE FOURTH SEAL

In Matt. 24, Mark 13, and Luke 21 Jesus instructed us with over thirty commands to be *observant*, to *see*, and to be *watchful*. The reason he instructs us to be watchful is because in the Gospel accounts, he gives us a number of signs. We will only see them if we watch.

"Watch" is a misunderstood word. Jesus instructed his disciples to "watch and pray" on the night he was betrayed. This is a wonderful analogy of what watching in the Tribulation is like. Jesus had taken his three closest disciples with him deeper into the Garden of Gethsemane that night. He then asked them to "keep watch with him." When he returned to them, they had fallen asleep. Jesus woke them and rebuked them.

> So, you men could not keep watch with Me for one hour?
> *Keep watching and praying that you may not enter into*
> *temptation*; the spirit is willing, but the flesh is weak. (Matt.
> 26:40-41 NASB, emphasis mine)

Jesus instructed them (and us) to be continually watching and praying so we might not enter into temptation. All the disciples fled, and Peter committed apostasy by denying Jesus. Our Lord was only too aware that when the moment of testing came, it could not be *humanly* overcome.

Jesus's prayer in the Garden has been great comfort to me and to all who struggle conforming to the Will of the Father. "My Father, if it is possible, let this cup pass from Me; yet not as I will, but as You will" (Matt. 26:39 NASB). If the sinless Son of God struggled in this way, it should not surprise us that we also wonder how we will overcome.

Jesus's words "the spirit is willing, but the flesh is weak" hold the clue. It will not be humanly possible to overcome. Our flesh is too weak to overcome on our own (no matter how we try to strengthen it). But, and this is the encouraging part, the spirit within us is willing, yes, willing to do the Father's Will. Only by prayer can we tap into his Spirit to empower it.

Prayer is of obvious help! But what use is watching? Judas and the Temple guards were coming up the path from the city to the garden with lit torches. If the disciples had been awake and watching, they would have seen this procession coming up the hill and could have prepared themselves for the confrontation that was about to come upon them. This is analogous to the coming of the Antichrist upon the world.

118

The most significant sign, the sign of the man of sin's revealing, occurs at the midpoint of the Tribulation:

Therefore *when you **see** the abomination of desolation* which was spoken of through Daniel the prophet, standing in the holy place (let the reader understand), then those who are in Judea must flee to the mountains. (Matt. 24:15–16 NASB, emphasis mine)

Jesus wants us to be watchful so we can see the signs he has warned us about. These signs form a chronology (Gk. *chronos*) which Paul assumes Christians will understand (1 Thess. 5:1). Paul assumes we will be familiar with the chronology of the end times because it was given to us by Jesus in the Gospel accounts. Paul expects us to have committed these signs to memory to help ourselves and others. Again, the churches that are organized as the Church of Acts will have an incredible advantage knowing where they are in the chronology of end times. They will not be taken by surprise by the Great Tribulation that immediately follows this event.

Churchgoers will need to decide how to react to this event (the Great Tribulation). Will they go into hiding or face down the Antichrist and testify? When believers see this horrible sign of the Abomination of Desolation set up upon the newly rebuilt Temple of God, they can know that the *physical* return of our Savior to the earth is only *forty-two months away*. That is all the time that the Antichrist is given authority. Believers can also know that the resurrection and *prewrath rapture* will occur even sooner. With that little time remaining, what should their strategy be: **survivalist** or **revivalist**? Jesus inspired John to quote Jeremiah 15:2 in this passage in Revelation:

If anyone is *destined for captivity,* to captivity he goes; if anyone kills with the sword, with the sword he must be killed. *Here is the perseverance and the faith of the saints.* (Rev. 13:10 NASB, emphasis mine)

Trying to be a ***survivalist*** will be pointless. Many are destined for captivity or death. True faith is shining the light of Jesus even in the midst of persecution. This will be especially important to demonstrate and model before our weaker brothers and sisters.

In the parable of the talents, Jesus also taught that those that hide their great treasure (the gospel) will be cast into outer darkness. To me this implies they won't be raptured. Hiding doesn't seem an option.

However, Jesus also instructs us to be as wise as serpents and as gentle as doves. He doesn't expect churches to be foolish. In Matt. 10, Jesus sent out his disciples as a foreshadow of his instructions to us for the Great Tribulation:

Behold, I send you out as sheep in the midst of wolves; so be shrewd as serpents and innocent as doves. *But beware of men,* for they will hand you over to the courts and scourge you in their synagogues . . . Brother will betray brother to death, and a father his child; and children will rise up against parents and cause them to be put to death. (Matt. 10:16-17, 21 NASB, emphasis mine)

Jesus wants us to beware of men. This will be a time when knowing the voice of the Holy Spirit will be of utmost importance. Only the Spirit's guidance will help Christians navigate the minefield of those days. Additionally, Jesus gave a couple additional specific instructions that I find helpful:

> And whatever city or village you enter, inquire who is worthy in it, and stay at his house until you leave that city. As you enter the house, give it your greeting. If the house is worthy, give it your blessing of peace. (Matt. 10:11-13 NASB)

> But whenever they persecute you in one city, flee to the next (Matt. 10:23 NASB)

Jesus expects Christians to be on the move, traveling from city to city as the persecution intensifies. He also expects them to network with other believers within each town and city.

> *Be Thou my Breastplate, my Sword for the fight;*
> *Be Thou my whole Armor, be Thou my true Might;*
> *Be Thou my soul's Shelter, be Thou my strong Tow'r,*
> *O raise Thou me heav'nward, great Pow'r of my pow'r*[18]

## THE SPIRIT AND APOCALYPTIC EVANGELISM

During those days of the Great Tribulation, Christians will have two advantages in evangelism that we currently don't have. First, God is going to pour out his Spirit on all flesh prior to the Great and Terrible Day of the Lord (Joel 2:28). The unsaved will be especially receptive to the gospel message.

---

[18] Be Thou My Vision, Verse Three, traditional Irish hymn "Rop tú mo Baile," English text by Eleanor Hull

Second, we will be able to utilize fulfilled prophetic events for evangelism. The pretribulation rapture theory's concept of imminence will disarm the church during the Tribulation if they don't realize this fact. Prophecies fulfilled before your eyes can have an awesome impact on evangelism. If one believes there are no more prophecies to be fulfilled (as with a belief in imminence), they will miss this enormous opportunity.

Apocalyptic evangelism is a form of evangelism that uses *fulfilled prophecy as a basis to prove the claims of Jesus* and the Bible. This technique was most dramatically utilized by Peter in his sermon on the day of Pentecost as seen in Acts 2:

> This is what was spoken of through the prophet Joel: "And it shall be in the last days," God says, "That *I will pour forth of My Spirit on all mankind; and your sons and your daughters shall prophesy,* and your young men shall see visions, and your old men shall dream dreams; Even on My bond-slaves, both men and women, I will in those days pour forth of My Spirit and they shall prophesy. And I will grant wonders in the sky above and signs on the earth below, blood, and fire, and vapor of smoke. The sun will be turned into darkness and the moon into blood, before the great and glorious *day of the Lord* shall come. And it shall be that everyone who calls on the name of the Lord will be saved." (Acts 2:16–21 NASB, emphasis mine)

First, Peter identified the prophecy that the Israelites were seeing fulfilled before their eyes: the pouring out of God's Spirit. Peter also mentioned the supernatural darkening of the sky upon Jesus's crucifixion as "just as you yourselves know" (Acts 2:22). Peter then quoted a second prophecy from Psalm 16, which they would have recognized:

> I saw the Lord always in my presence; For He is at my right hand, so that I will not be shaken. "Therefore my heart was glad and my tongue exulted; Moreover my flesh also will live in hope; Because *You will not abandon my soul to Hades, nor allow Your Holy One to undergo decay.* You have made known to me the ways of life; You will make me full of gladness with Your presence." (Acts 2:25–28 NASB, emphasis mine)

All those in attendance knew the rumors of Jesus having risen from the dead. Peter showed how this prophecy from Psalms could only apply to Jesus and not to its author David. The result of Peter's sermon (and the working of the Holy Spirit through the Word) was that three thousand were saved and baptized on that one day.

*Believers will most likely have the opportunity to utilize this technique in the coming years* as they see end-time prophecies fulfilled. They will be able to say, "This is what God's Word said would take place." It will be a powerful evangelistic tool; *if* those Christians *believe* that there will be prophecies to fulfill prior to Jesus's return and *recognize* the prophecies when they are being fulfilled before their eyes.

## MARTYRDOM AND THE CHURCH OF THE FIFTH SEAL

The Great Tribulation, will be one of the most significant events in world history. It will be *a time of decision*. The *eternal destiny* of much of the world will hang in a balance. Most Christians will be forced to choose between physical death (and spiritual life) or physical life (and spiritual death). This will be a monumental choice. How Christians handle this public decision will have an *eternal impact* on those watching: both unbelievers and those whose faith might be weak. In the letter to Sardis (the Church of the Fifth Seal), Jesus addresses this concern:

> Wake up, and *strengthen the things that remain, which were about to die*; for *I have not found your deeds completed in the sight of My God*. So remember what you have received and heard; and keep it and repent. (Rev. 3:2–3 NASB, emphasis mine)

Jesus's command is to *strengthen the things that were about to die*. This may have a personal application (strengthening our own faith), but it also has a corporate application. By the testimony of our words and deeds (martyrdom), we can strengthen the resolve and faith of those watching, both unbelievers and believers. It will be the greatest time of witness the world has ever seen. Christians may have been through a lot during the first years of the Tribulation, but God's Word is telling them that their deeds are not completed. They still need to witness during this most significant time. That witness may (and probably will) include *martyrdom*.

God's promise of reward to those that suffer is great. "He who overcomes will thus be *clothed in white garments*; and I will *not erase his name* from the *book of life*, and *I will confess his name before My Father and before His angels*" (Rev. 3:5 NASB, emphasis mine). These are the ones who will participate in the wedding supper of the Lamb. A momentary trial that is overcome will lead to this greatest of rewards. This is so important to keep in mind because eventually most Christians will be handed over to the Antichrist forces. Jesus's instructions are clear:

124

> Do not be afraid of those who kill the body and after that have
> no more that they can do. But I will warn you whom to fear:
> fear the One who, after He has killed, has authority to cast
> into hell; yes, I tell you, fear Him! (Luke 12:4-5 NASB)

We are not to fear a martyr's death, and in the Great Tribulation that is the most likely scenario. Jesus wants us to remember that he is returning and will have his reward with him! Regardless of what else happens, we are to maintain our testimony:

> Everyone who confesses me before men, the Son of Man will
> confess him also before the angels of God; but he who denies
> me before men will be denied before the angels of God. And
> everyone who speaks a word against the Son of Man, it will
> be forgiven him; but *he who blasphemes against the Holy
> Spirit, it will not be forgiven him.* When they bring you before
> the synagogues and the rulers and the authorities, do not
> worry about how or what you are to speak in your defense, or
> what you are to say; *for the Holy Spirit will teach you in that
> very hour what you ought to say.*" (Luke 12:8-12, clarification
> and emphasis mine)

Notice the definition of the blasphemy of the Holy Spirit is given in this context; in the context of confessing or denying Jesus in the hour of decision. The Holy Spirit will give us what it is we are and are not to say. To blaspheme and ignore him at that moment is the unforgivable sin! This is a point the church has vastly misunderstood about Jesus's teaching.

*High King of Heaven, my victory won*

*May I reach Heaven's joys, O bright Heav'n's Sun*

*Heart of my own heart, whate'er befall*

*Still be my Vision, O Ruler of all*[19]

## FORGIVE US OUR DEBTS AS WE FORGIVE

*Forgiveness* will also be a means of testimony. Horrific things will be done by the forces of the Antichrist. We are still commanded to forgive the way Jesus did as he hung dying on the cross. The testimony of former Nazi concentration camp survivor Corrie ten Boom highlights the power of forgiveness. Her story involves forgiving, years later, one of her Nazi tormentors:

"I, who had spoken so glibly of forgiveness, fumbled in my pocketbook rather than take that hand [of her tormentor]. He would not remember me, of course—how could he remember one prisoner among those thousands of women? But I remembered him and the leather crop swinging from his belt. It was the first time since my release that I had been face to face with one of my captors and my blood seemed to freeze."

"You mentioned Ravensbrück in your talk," he was saying. "I was a guard in there." No, he did not remember me.

"But since that time," he went on, "I have become a Christian. I know that God has forgiven me for the cruel things I did there, but I would like to hear it from your lips as well. *Fräulein*"—again the hand came out—"will you forgive me?" . . . "And so woodenly, mechanically, I thrust my hand into the one stretched out to me.

---

And as I did, an incredible thing took place. The current started in my shoulder, raced down my arm, sprang into our joined hands. And then this healing warmth seemed to flood my whole being, bringing tears to my eyes."

"I forgive you, brother!" I cried. "With all my heart!" —Corrie ten Boom[20] (clarification mine)

We, too, need to be as willing to practice forgiveness of others, even after horrendous things have happened to us. God understands, and he will help us be more like Jesus.

### THE CHURCH OF THE SIXTH SEAL

But those days (the days of the great tribulation) will be cut short, most likely by the darkening of the sun and moon (the sixth seal). This will be a time of great terror for the unrighteous, but a sign of rejoicing for the saints. Jesus tells us:

> But when these things [the darkening of the sun, etc.] begin to take place, straighten up and lift up your heads, because your redemption is drawing near. (Luke 21:28 NASB, clarification mine)

While the rest of the world is hiding in caves, Christians are to lift their heads because Jesus's *parousia* has almost come.

---

[20] "Corrie Ten Boom on Forgiveness," Guideposts, last modified: unknown, accessed April 21, 2016, https://www.guideposts.org/inspiration/stories-of-hope/guideposts-classics-corrie-ten-boom-on-forgiveness?nopaging=1

The sixth seal reminds us dramatically of the Rapture, and reminds us that false rapture theories are dangerous. They have the potential to lull the church to sleep; sleeping saints cannot be watchful. The time to wake up is not during the Great Tribulation when the choice of life and death is set before them. The time to wake up is *now* so that they (we) can help awaken the church.

*The Gospel in the End Times Ministries* is dedicated to awakening the church. I suggest you to volunteer to join this worthy effort at nelson@thegospelintheendtimes.com.

> **The time to awaken the church from the error of false rapture theories is now.**

Proper understanding of the Rapture and its timing, at the present time, may lead a person to strengthen their faith to evangelize now and to participate in the resurrection and rapture later.

### SUMMARY

Even the apostle Peter needed to be reminded that it would take *agapao* love of Jesus for him to tolerate the trials ahead and overcome them. Peter bragged to Jesus on the night he was betrayed that even if all the other disciples committed apostasy, he would not. That did not turn out so well. After Peter's fall from grace, Jesus asked him if he still thought he loved Jesus "more than these" (the other disciples). We must not be as presumptuous as Peter was. Our love of Jesus and our work in preparation of the church must be our number-one focus. All of the members of the church need to be involved in this preparation so that each of us can be overcomers in the days ahead, as we watch for the signs Jesus has given us related to his coming. We need to prepare individually and teach this in our churches.

As you have considered the biblical evidence in this book, you have probably come to the conclusion that the church will face the Tribulation and the Antichrist prior to being rescued in a prewrath rapture. And after reading the suggestions for preparation in this chapter, you may be realizing that you may face your own personal tribulation coming to grips with what must be done to properly endure it and be a witness to others.

Many of our readers have spent a career in ministry espousing a rapture theory that Christians will be spared from the hard times to come. Now that we know with biblical certainty that believers will face the Antichrist, a decision must be made that only you can answer:

**Will you risk your reputation, career, and friendships to save the souls of those under your leadership by renouncing escapist theories?**

May God grant all of us the wisdom, strength, and courage to follow him.

*Be Thou my Vision, O Lord of my heart*
*Naught be all else to me, save that Thou art*
*Be thou my wisdom and Thou my true word*
*I ever with Thee and Thou with me, Lord*[21]

---

[21] *Be Thou My Vision*, Verse One and Two, traditional Irish hymn "Rop tú mo Baile," English text by Eleanor Hull

Made in the USA
Monee, IL
21 December 2022

23280506R00083